BOOKS BY ANTHONY F. C. WALLACE

King of the Delawares
Culture and Personality
Religion: An Anthropological View
Death and Rebirth of the Seneca
Rockdale: The Growth of an American Village
Social Context of Innovation
St. Clair: A Nineteenth-Century Coal Town

THE LONG, BITTER TRAIL

THE LONG, BITTER TRAIL

Andrew Jackson and the Indians

ANTHONY F. C.
WALLACE

A CRITICAL ISSUE

CONSULTING EDITOR: ERIC FONER

 HILL AND WANG

A division of Farrar, Straus and Giroux / New York

First edition, 1993
Designed by Fritz Metsch

LIBRARY OF CONGRESS CATALOGING-IN-PUBLICATION DATA
Wallace, Anthony F. C.
The long bitter trail : Andrew Jackson and the Indians / Anthony
F. C. Wallace ; consulting editor, Eric Foner. — 1st ed.
p.   cm. — (A Critical Issue series)
Includes index.
1. Jackson, Andrew, 1767–1845—Relations with Indians.   2. Indians
of North America—Removal.   3. Indians of North America—Government
relations—1789–1869.   I. Foner, Eric.   II. Title.   III. Series.
E381.W29   1993   323.1′197073′09034—dc20   92-32609 CIP

93 - 1583

TO

CHERYL

AND

JOSEPH

PREFACE

The Indian Removal Act of 1830 was passed by Congress and signed into law by President Andrew Jackson well over 150 years ago; its antecedents and consequences are woven into the very fabric of our national existence. This book offers an interpretive account of the process by which many of the Native Americans who resided in the states east of the Mississippi River were deprived of their lands and their liberties and deposited in an "Indian territory" in what is now the state of Oklahoma.

In writing such an account, it is necessary to establish some conventions about the use of language. Although the term "Native Americans" is more appropriate today than "Indians," in the idiom of the nineteenth century the word "Indians" is invariably employed. Rather than rigidly display in my own text a different word from that which appears in the sources, I have chosen to treat the two terms as interchangeable synonyms. Tribal designations are also awkward; although many authorities use the adjectival form of a tribal name as its noun form, this usage is not consistent with all tribes (one might say "the Seneca attended the treaty" but would not say "the Creek attended the treaty," preferring the plural "Creeks" in that case). I have elected to use the noun plural in all references to tribes as groups. There is a problem with the word "civilize" and its derivatives. Nineteenth-century writers regularly refer to at-

tempts to persuade Native Americans to speak English, convert
to Christianity, and adopt white customs as laudable efforts to
"civilize" them; some tribes (particularly those of central interest
in this account) were labeled "civilized tribes." Such usage
undoubtedly reflects a high degree of cultural arrogance, but
to bowdlerize the language of the past with contemporary
euphemisms would distort the social reality of the period.
Another terminological problem is the word "treaty," which was
then used to refer both to a conference and to the written
agreement eventually produced. I have followed the earlier
usage. Geographical names also present difficulties: for instance,
states now include land which in the period under study were
official territories, or public lands of the United States. For the
sake of simplicity, I have sometimes referred to locations in
terms familiar to twentieth-century readers.

Although this little book is intended mainly for students
of history and others primarily interested in this historical
event, the writer is an anthropologist and cannot resist
seeing events, as well as cultures, in some sort of comparative
perspective. One comparative observation is unavoidable.
The removal of inconveniently located ethnic groups and their
resettlement in out-of-the-way places is, and has been for
thousands of years, a common phenomenon in the history of
states and empires. The removal of the Eastern Indians is a
typical case. Nations all over the world today face the need
to find ways of organizing diversity instead of trying to remove it.

I want to express my appreciation to several persons who
have helped me in writing this book. My particular gratitude
goes to the Library of the American Philosophical Society; its
director, Edward Carter III; reference librarian, Roy Goodman;
and manuscripts librarian, Beth Carroll-Horrocks. Invaluable
editorial commentary was supplied by Arthur Wang and Eric
Foner. My daughter-in-law, Paige Wallace, prepared the two
excellent maps of Native American locations before and after

removal. And to my typist, Judy Murray, I extend thanks for her patience in reading my handwriting and processing one draft after another.

Rockdale
April 30, 1992

CONTENTS

THE LONG, BITTER TRAIL

THE HUNGER FOR INDIAN LAND

IN ANDREW JACKSON'S AMERICA

ANDREW Jackson was a young lawyer of twenty-one when in 1788 he moved to Nashville, the principal town in the Cumberland Valley in what is now the state of Tennessee. The Cumberland Valley had been purchased from the Cherokee Indians only three years before. It was very much a frontier region, still subject to occasional raids from hostile natives. Fortunes were being made and lost in land speculations, trading in horses and slaves, betting on horse races, storekeeping, and cotton growing, and the young lawyer tried it all. He soon married Rachel Donelson Robards, the daughter of a powerful local clan, but unwittingly and unfortunately the ceremony was performed before Rachel's divorce from her first husband was final. The devoted couple had to be legally remarried later, and gossip about the "scandal" plagued them for years. Jackson's fortunes ebbed and flowed, but he eventually secured a prosperous cotton plantation on the outskirts of Nashville, The Hermitage, a one-square-mile estate which remained his residence for the rest of his life.

As a member of the Nashville gentry, he naturally took part in the political life of the area. In 1796, when Tennessee was about to be admitted into the Union, he became a member of the convention that wrote a constitution for the new state, and in the same year was elected to serve as the first representative to Congress from the state of Tennessee. He entered the U.S. Senate in 1797, but resigned after one year, pleading financial difficulties. Soon, however, he was appointed a judge of the Superior Court of the state and stayed a member of that body until 1804.

In 1802, Jackson was elected major general of the Tennessee militia, and he retained that post through the War of 1812. At the end of that war, by defeating the Creek Indians in Alabama in 1814 and repulsing the British before New Orleans in 1815, he had achieved national prominence as the only American military hero of that inconclusive conflict. Appointed a commissioner to treat with the Southern Indians, in the six years immediately after the war he was able, personally, to force cessions of land upon both friendly and hostile tribes, and to begin the process of removal of the Southern Indians to the "Indian territory" west of the Mississippi. Jackson's success as treaty commissioner from 1815 to 1820 was phenomenal: in those years he and his fellow commissioners persuaded the tribes, by fair means or foul, to sell to the United States a major portion of their lands in the Southeast, including a fifth of Georgia, half of Mississippi, and most of the land area of Alabama.

Andrew Jackson had a personal financial interest in some of the lands whose purchase he arranged. His attention focused particularly on an area in northern Alabama, south of that part of the Tennessee River known as Muscle Shoals, acquired from the Cherokees in a treaty surrounded by allegations of fraud. The Senate, in fact, refused to ratify the treaty and it had to be renegotiated. The lands south of this stretch of river were in frontier times seen as a prospectively lucrative site for agricultural development, and efforts had been under way to acquire it from its Native American owners, the Cherokees, since the 1780s. More recently, the land south of the Shoals had been recognized as prime cotton acreage. Jackson and his troops had repeatedly marched through there during the war. Now that cotton prices were rising, and old cotton land to the east was reaching exhaustion, the demand for accessible agricultural land like that in northern Alabama had become intense. By the time the cession was completed, in 1816, 10,000 squatters had entered the territory now being described as the future "Garden of America."

Andrew Jackson and his nephew by marriage John Coffee, a former fellow officer in the war against the Creeks in 1813 and 1814, were at the center of the "Alabama fever." Jackson in late 1816 used his influence in Washington to have Coffee appointed head government surveyor of the Alabama land cessions. In this post, Coffee was in a position to know exactly where the most valuable lands were, and he made his fortune by it. At the suggestion of his Uncle Andrew, it is said, Coffee made an agreement with the Land Office clerks to receive half of any bribes they took for giving information about land or aiding in its acquisition. Coffee also took care of his relatives. Among other enterprises, he formed a land company whose shares were divided among Tennessee and Philadelphia speculators; Andrew Jackson was one of them. In 1818 Jackson bought land on his own near the Shoals (with no one bidding against him), and in the same year Coffee bought eighty-three tracts totaling 16,000 acres. The officially recorded value of these lands was $76,000 (at $4.75 an acre), but comparable land in the same area was selling for $40 an acre and some for as much as $78 an acre. Jackson later also acquired a 2,700-acre plantation in Mississippi on erstwhile Indian land.

The hunger for Indian land was most intense in the Southern slave-owning states, and Jackson as a politician generally reflected Southern economic interests. He became the political prime mover of the Indian-removal process. In 1824 he ran unsuccessfully for President on the Democratic ticket. In 1828 he tried again, and won, and one of his first actions as President was to call, in his inaugural address in 1829, for the passage of a Removal Act that would effectively dislodge the Native Americans—and especially the Southern tribes—from their ancestral lands east of the Mississippi River and colonize them in an Indian territory west of the Mississippi. The Act was passed in 1830, and during the remainder of his presidency, and for several years thereafter, the government proceeded to persuade—with force when necessary—the tribes to "voluntarily" surrender their territories and emigrate to allotted tracts, primarily in what is now the state of Oklahoma.

In all this mania for the land of the Native Americans, Jackson himself does not stand out as the greediest of speculators. He took care of himself, to be sure, and he was always ready to reward family, friends, and political constituents, but he was also concerned to develop the country by expanding its agriculture and commerce. By the time of his death in 1845 (after virtually all the Southern Indians had been removed), he had managed to amass an extensive estate, including the well-furnished mansion at The Hermitage, two plantations, 161 slaves, a valuable stable of fifty horses, and hundreds of head of livestock. He was in his financial dealings a typical man of his time, and by action, precept, and example he fed the land fever of others.

But although Jackson was the most visible, forceful, and effective exponent of the white man's desire to acquire Indian land, the source of his own and others' land hunger lay in larger processes of economic change. The appetite for Indian land in the American South in the 1820s and '30s was whetted by economic events outside the region, in Great Britain and the northern part of the United States. There an industrial revolution was under way. Steam engines had been developed to pump water out of coal mines, making access to the deeper veins for the first time practicable; steam engines now supplied power for factories, permitting a concentration of production in cities rather than in the old dispersed pattern along country streams that turned waterwheels; steam engines powered boats on the waters and steam locomotives drew trains of cars on land, opening up for economic development (along with a network of canals) new regions hitherto virtually inaccessible. And to supply the increasing need for iron and steel, English blast furnaces were now able to substitute for charcoal a seemingly inexhaustible supply of coke, cheaply made from soft coal; and American iron works (after the introduction of the hot blast in the late 1830s) were able to employ another seemingly inexhaustible supply of fuel, Pennsylvania anthracite.

In Great Britain, the centerpiece of the Industrial Revolution was cotton manufacturing. Large factories, powered by water or steam, crammed with long lines of automatic spinning and weaving machines, spewed out enormous quantities of yarn and cloth made from American raw cotton. British cotton goods were sold all over the world as the British Empire extended its global economic grip, and as a result the demand for American cotton was voracious.

America produced, in the mid-1830s, about 400 million pounds of cotton per year, most of it exported to Great Britain. According to one estimate, America sold abroad in 1836 about 384 million pounds of raw cotton, which amounted to two-thirds of all the cotton produced for export in the world. Upland Georgia cotton, a variety of middling quality, cost about ten cents a pound to produce; it sold on an average for sixteen cents a pound, but prices could go as high as forty-four cents a pound; a single acre would produce a crop of about two hundred pounds. A 500-acre cotton plantation thus could expect to make a profit on the order of $6,000 a year—a very large sum in those days.

The worldwide demand for manufactured cotton goods was enormous. In England, France, and the United States, about eight pounds of cotton cloth per capita was consumed each year, and although far less cotton was used in the non-industrialized countries, it was estimated that worldwide consumption of manufactured cotton goods amounted to two pounds per capita per annum. With a world population of about 450 million at that time, the annual consumption of cotton goods was about 900 million pounds, nearly half of it made from raw cotton grown in the American South.

Americans of all sorts, in all kinds of places, were obsessed with Southern cotton. The hunger for new cotton lands affected all classes of Southern society. Not merely prospective growers of plantation cotton caught the "Alabama fever," but also land speculators, and settlers who expected to make their fortunes in subsidiary activities on which the plantations depended— millwrights, blacksmiths, and other artisans of all kinds, doctors and lawyers, teamsters and steamboat captains, storekeepers and small farmers and railway workers. The demand for raw cotton was also increasing in the Northern United States, particularly in New England and Pennsylvania, where American cotton mills were beginning to compete with the British in the expanding American market for cotton goods. The Northern factories were aided, to be sure, by a protective tariff, which drove up the cost of British goods in the North as well as the South, and was leading to a bitter interregional conflict over federal tariff policy.

The increasing resentment in the South against the protective tariff was only one factor in the rise of a separatist sentiment that was becoming increasingly virulent. Particularly in Georgia, there was real bitterness against the federal government (which alone had the constitutional authority to hold treaties with the Native Americans and to purchase their lands) for its failure to remove the Indians. It had promised to do so as long ago as 1802, when Georgia relinquished to the United States its claim to sovereignty over what became the states of Alabama and Mississippi. The promise to purchase all the Native American land in Georgia, turn it over to the state, and transport the Indians elsewhere still remained partially unfulfilled when the Removal Act was finally passed, after much debate, in 1830.

The urge to convert "unused" Indian land into commercially productive cotton fields affected not only the white folks but the Native Americans themselves. Among the Southern Indians particularly, there was a recognized social class called "half-

breeds," distinguished from the "full-bloods" by some degree
of white ancestry, usually on the father's side. Many of these
half-breeds were sired by men of property who had taken
refuge, or made their fortunes in, Indian country, had married
Indian—or part-Indian—women, and had raised their children
in homes where English was spoken. These children were sent
to mission schools or even to white academies, where they
received anything from a basic acquaintance with the three R's
to an education in the classics and advanced training in one of
the professions. Although they identified themselves as Indians
in a native community where one's tribal and clan membership
were inherited from the mother, they emulated their white
cousins in economic behavior. For a considerable number of
half-breeds, the form this emulation took—or perhaps competition would be a better word—was to establish a cotton plantation, complete with mansion house, livestock, and black slaves.

One of the most successful of the Native American plantation
owners was the Cherokee chief John Ross (1790–1866). His
father was a Loyalist of Scottish origin who fled the persecution
of the rebels during the Revolution, married a Cherokee woman
(herself actually of only one-quarter Indian descent), and
remained with the tribe after independence. John Ross was
educated at a white academy in Tennessee but returned to live
in the Cherokee country. During the War of 1812, being literate
in English as well as fluent in Cherokee, he volunteered to serve
as adjutant officer to a regiment of Cherokee warriors recruited
by Andrew Jackson to fight against the Creeks, who had joined
the British. He took part with Jackson and Coffee in the bloody
battle at Horseshoe Bend on the Tallapoosa River, where Ross's
regiment played a major role in the slaughter of over five
hundred Creek fighters and the sacking of their main fortified
town.

In the years after the war, proud, aristocratic in manner,
statesmanlike in policy, Ross became a man of great influence
in the Cherokee nation. He established his own plantation in

Georgia, at the head of the Coosa River near the Alabama line, where he served as federal postmaster and operated a lucrative ferry worth $1,000 per year in income. It was a substantial establishment on about three hundred acres, including a large two-story family residence, seventy feet long, boasting twenty glass windows and a covered porch running the length of it. There was an overseer's house, three cabins for his twenty or so slaves, a building where circuit preachers regularly held Methodist services, various barns and stables, a blacksmith shop, and fruit orchards. "Head of Coosa" was appraised, after he was driven out of it, at about $20,000. John Ross was not wealthy on the scale of an Andrew Jackson—but he was prosperous. Favoring the "civilization" of Native Americans in their ancestral territories, he supported the introduction of missionary academies and training schools for artisans. He was a prime mover in creating the Cherokee republican constitution, modeled after that of the United States, in 1827. He was, however, as one of the two principal chiefs established in the new government, the leader of the major faction that opposed Jackson and his removal policy. His opposition, of course, proved to be unsuccessful, and his former association with Andrew Jackson did him no good: an attempt was made on his life by a white man, his plantation was seized and sold in the Georgia lottery, he was briefly arrested and jailed, he was forced to organize the removal of most of the tribe, and his Indian wife, Quatie, died in Arkansas in 1839 during the emigration so aptly called "the trail of tears."

Yet John Ross did not give up the struggle to advance the fortunes of the Cherokees. He served as principal chief of the united Cherokee nation in Indian territory until his death in 1866. And he built a new cotton plantation, worked (until emancipation) by numerous slaves.

John Ross was, in a sense, the mirror image of Andrew Jackson, a gentleman of the Old South, stamped on the Indian side of the American coin. And what white Georgia feared most was the rise of men like John Ross. It was not the "savagery" of the Indians that land-hungry whites dreaded; it was their "civilization."

The consequences of the trans-Mississippi removal of the Southern Indians, and to a lesser extent of the Northern Indians as well, were momentous. The United States acquired millions of acres of fertile Southern land, which it sold at little or no profit to speculators and settlers, thereby in effect subsidizing the expansion of the cotton industry and the slave system along with it. The rapidly increasing population in the North also moved westward. For the Native Americans who were relocated in the Indian territory, the removal was of course an immediate disaster, costly in lives and wealth.

But it was a disaster that never really ended. The government thereafter pursued the same policy of buying Native American lands and relocating Native American tribes as the nation moved westward. The Indian territory (as did other reservations) became a vast, poverty-stricken concentration camp for dispossessed Native Americans, administered by a federal bureaucracy—the Bureau of Indian Affairs, created by Jackson's presidential directive—that largely controlled the local economy, the local police, and the local schools.

It is remarkable how little attention has been paid to the removal of the 1830s, and the events consequent upon it, by general historians of the United States. Despite the labors of a number of specialists in Indian history, the authors of textbooks and scholarly treatises that profess a national view have virtually ignored the Indian wars and removals of the post-colonial era. The Indians were big news in the seventeenth and eighteenth centuries; Francis Parkman memorialized their savage exploits during their wars against the French and the British. But the Native Americans appear only briefly as tiny blips on the screen of nineteenth-century history, unfriendly but fortunately feeble opponents of the manifest destiny that Jackson and his colleagues worked so ardently to fulfill, scarcely slowing the inevitable march of the redeemer nation to the Pacific. Attention

has been lavished instead on the political and economic restruc-
turing of America, on Jacksonian democracy, on the centrist vs.
separatist issue as it affected the banking system, tariff policy,
and the extension of slavery into states only recently liberated
from thralldom to their aboriginal occupants.

A few examples of this tendency to trivialize both the Native
Americans and the importance of their land cessions and
subsequent confinement on government-managed reservations
will suffice. In Frederick Jackson Turner's widely read work,
The Frontier in American History (1920), based on an earlier (1893)
essay, the Indians' role is summarized as a "consolidating agent.
. . . The Indian was a common danger, demanding united
action." Arthur Schlesinger, Jr.'s Pulitzer prize-winning *The Age
of Jackson* (1945) barely notices Native Americans (and then
merely as objects of missionary zeal) and does not mention the
removal of the Indians at all. The Seminole War is ignored. No
general entry for "Indians" or "Native Americans" is to be found
in the index. Allan Nevins and Henry Steele Commager in their
widely read textbook, *A Short History of the United States*, disparage
the Native Americans as being "too few and too backward," and
too poorly armed, to impede the westward advance of civilization. Furthermore, "they had shown little capacity to subdue
nature, and as they lived mainly by hunting and fishing, their
resources were precarious" (5th edition, 1966). No mention is
made of the contrary fact that many Indian populations, particularly those in the East, lived mainly by agriculture in pre-
Columbian times.

Although general historians have not always paid much
attention to Native Americans, it would be unfair to say that
the historical profession as a whole has either ignored or
Parkmanized the Indians. Some of Turner's students went on
to do important research on Indian subjects, and there have
been a number of distinguished historians who have specialized
in the field, including most recently such persons as James
Axtel, William Cronon, Wilbur Jacobs, Francis Jennings, Howard Lamar, Francis Paul Prucha, and Wilcomb Washburn. And

of course there have been excellent studies with a more narrowly tribal or regional focus, of which the contributions of Grant Foreman and Angie Debo are most widely known for the Southeast and Oklahoma.

In this connection, it is necessary to mention the fascinating psychohistorical study by Michael Paul Rogin, *Fathers and Children: Andrew Jackson and the Subjugation of the American Indian* (1975). Rogin presents a psychoanalytic interpretation of Jackson's own ambivalent motivations, and by extension those of his contemporaries. Basing his work on extensive reading of primary sources, Rogin argues that Jacksonian Americans unconsciously regarded the "Indian" as an attractive infantile being, freely acting out the sexual and aggressive tendencies that proper "civilized" men had to repress or otherwise defend themselves against. The white man in his heart wanted to be like the Indian; therefore, the Indian had to be removed to get temptation out of the way. It is an intriguing theory, and may indeed apply to Jackson and some others, but not necessarily to the whole of America. In any case, it does not disallow the operation of other motives—particularly greed, revenge, and guilt—in the process of Indian removal. As John Ross once observed, "The perpetrator of a wrong never forgives his victims."

In so brief a work as this, it will not be possible to review in full detail the Indian wars and removals of the Jacksonian epoch. But the book does aim to achieve some sort of balance of attention, looking at both the land-hungry white Americans and their Native American victims. And it tries to place the conflict between them, and its tragic resolution, in the context of the changing worlds in which both sides lived.

THE CHANGING WORLDS
OF THE NATIVE AMERICANS

LIKE the Europeans, the Native Americans lived in rapidly changing societies. Their ancestors had entered North America from Siberia in several streams of migration, beginning tens of thousands of years ago and ending well before the arrival of Europeans. As they spread southward, finally reaching the southern tip of South America, they adapted to the different zones of climate and vegetation, and developed—as did other peoples in Africa, Asia, Australia, Europe, and the Pacific Islands—increasingly distinct cultures and languages. Some of them, particularly in the region from what is now northern Mexico south to Peru, pursued a long course of cultural evolution parallel to that followed by the great civilizations of other continents, first developing agriculture (probably a female innovation), then creating dams, irrigation, and metallurgy, city-states, and eventually (certainly no later than A.D. 1000), highly organized empires (dominated by men). By the time Europeans first "discovered" the Americas, in the years from A.D. 1000 to 1500, advanced urban civilizations had existed for centuries in Mexico, Central America, and the Andean slopes, with irrigation agriculture, metallurgy, systems of writing and numerical calculation, centralized political power, elaborate religious beliefs and ceremonies, and far-flung trade networks. Of particular concern to us is the fact that the Mesoamerican city-states, by wars of conquest and by trade, had spread agricultural practices and some aspects of their political traditions far and wide, long before the arrival of Columbus.

Among those who benefited from the diffusion of agricultural practices, centuries before Columbus, were the people who lived east of the Mississippi River and south of the Great Lakes and St. Lawrence River valley. This vast land of temperate climate, extensive forests, and fertile meadows and prairies was inhabited by well over a million Native Americans. Although they were divided into dozens of tribes, each with its own unique language (although all these languages belonged to fewer than a dozen language groups), they all shared one basic feature: a subsistence economy based on the deliberate growing of corn and other vegetables in carefully tended gardens, supplemented by hunting and gathering. The Southern tribes, and particularly the Cherokees, the Choctaws, the Chickasaws, and the Creeks, with whom we shall be mostly concerned (along with a later offshoot of the Creeks known as the Seminoles), living between the Ohio River and the Gulf of Mexico, had larger, more urbanized populations, with more elaborate ceremonies and more impressive architecture, than the Northern horticulturists. But all were different in basic subsistence pattern from the peoples to the north of the Great Lakes, where the growing season was too short for corn, and to the far west of the Mississippi, where the high plains and cold mountains were also unfriendly to the Eastern style of horticulture. These Northern and Western tribes (with the exception of the Mexicanized Pueblo Indians of the Southwest) were therefore completely dependent on hunting and gathering for their food.

The eastern half of the United States was, in aboriginal times, almost entirely covered by forests. In what are now the states of Florida and Louisiana and the coastal and piedmont areas of Georgia, Alabama, and Mississippi, the trees were evergreens. To the north grew mixed broadleaf deciduous and evergreen species. East of the Mississippi, in what is now Illinois, prairie intruded, an eastern extension of the sea of grass that spread over much of the land west of the big river. Within this great forested region, however, along the edges of rivers and lakes, lay numerous grassy meadows. For hundreds of years before Columbus, Native Americans had built their villages in these natural clearings, raised corn and other vegetables, and hunted, fished, and gathered wild fruits, nuts, and maple syrup in the forests nearby, and to the north, especially in swamps around the Great Lakes, wild rice. Maize ("Indian corn") was the staple food throughout the region, except for some coastal areas and southern Florida, where seafood was predominant in the diet, and on the prairies, where the hunting of large herd animals like the buffalo assumed more importance.

The basic social and subsistence unit throughout the Eastern woodlands was the village. Each village was composed of a number of large communal houses, each occupied by a number of families, usually linked by matrilineal kinship. This meant that the women and their children belonged to a unilineal descent group, or clan (in technical jargon, a "sib"); the husbands were in a sense peripheral, being members of other clans. These clans were usually named after animal species important to the economy, such as the beaver or the deer, or symbolic of such virtues as speed, courage, or cunning, such as the wolf or the eagle, but there was no belief that the members of a clan were descended from their totem. The population of such villages ranged from a few hundred to a few thousand. The women cultivated garden plots in the meadows around or among the houses, working together clan by clan to plant, weed, and harvest the "Three Sisters" (corn, squash, and beans), and tobacco, which was smoked ceremonially. The women also managed the household, preserving, preparing, and cooking food, making pottery and baskets and clothing. The men helped to clear the fields, to raise and repair the houses; and they helped to provide food by hunting, trapping, and fishing. The prime hunting season was in the fall, after the corn had been harvested and the Green Corn ceremony, a thanksgiving ritual found everywhere in the Eastern woodlands, had been performed.

And everywhere, too, the men made war, in a never-ending cycle of revenge, or blood feud, between villages and tribes.

Although the basic subsistence technology of the Northeastern and Southeastern Indians was largely shared, there were significant differences between the two regions. One of these was in population. Various authorities have offered wildly disparate numbers, but a reasonable estimate of the Native American population of the Southeast—an area of about 350,000 square miles—at the time of first contact with Europeans is 1 million. After disease, war, and removal had taken their toll, the original population had been reduced by over 90 percent, to roughly 75,000. The original population of the Northeastern horticultural area, by most estimates, was considerably lower, and it was distributed over a much larger area. Part of the Northern region, the lower Ohio Valley, was for reasons that are obscure (perhaps it was the result of unrelenting warfare) almost uninhabited. There were pockets of dense population along the New England coast, where fishing groups might have local population densities as high as four persons per square mile, exceeding the average density of three per square mile in the Southeast.

A second major difference between the Southern and the Northern tribes had to do with the participation of men in the agricultural enterprise. In the North, men left the tending of the gardens entirely to the women, and these relatively small gardens produced little surplus beyond the needs of each village. Among the tribes of the Southeast, however, the men labored in large communal fields, raising corn and other vegetables, producing a surplus that was stored in communal granaries to be traded or eaten in time of need.

The third major difference between the Southern and Northern tribes was the more complex level of political organization in the South. The Native Americans of the Southeast were the heirs of a highly advanced pre-Columbian civilization, named by archaeologists the "Mississippian Tradition," which was ultimately related to the high cultures of Mexico and Central America. The variety of corn (Eastern flint) that they grew originated among the Maya of Guatemala; the Mississippian religious symbolism echoed Aztec motifs, presumably brought north by traders from the Valley of Mexico. And like the Maya and the Aztecs, the Middle Mississippians built large pyramidal ceremonial mounds, some as high as 100 feet. A major Middle Mississippian central area, with pyramid, plaza, residences, and a perimeter defended by palisades and moats, might have as many as forty thousand residents. All this implies a strong, centralized administrative authority. At its apex, about A.D. 1200, the Mississippian Tradition produced what anthropologist Charles Hudson, a specialist on the Southeastern Indians, has called, perhaps too enthusiastically, "the highest cultural achievement . . . in all of North America."

By the time Europeans arrived in numbers in the sixteenth century (perhaps after European diseases like smallpox and measles had already been introduced by occasional previous visitors), the Native Americans of the Southeast were no longer building temple mounds. But there remained a highly structured political unit, the chiefdom, and maybe even some nascent city-states. In these chiefdoms there was a clearly defined ranking system, based not so much on wealth as on heredity, age, and accomplishment. Symbols of rank included tattoos, special names or titles, prominent seating in the council house. In the colonial period, leaders of these quasi-states apparently did not have the authority of the high chiefs of earlier times, but enough of their power survived to enable Southern chiefdoms to mobilize thousands of men in military assaults against early European invaders.

Large towns, with palisaded fort, council house, regular streets, and a central plaza or court for playing the sacred ball game, were still being built well into the colonial period, and a tribe might also have a national ceremonial center located on the site of an ancient ceremonial mound. Related families still occupied traditional quarter-acre compounds, with winter and summer houses and outbuildings for storage of food, peltries and furs, and equipment. The Chickasaw winter house, to give an example, was circular, about twenty-five feet in diameter, thatch-roofed, the walls constructed of wattle and daub, white-washed inside and out. The summer house was a lighter structure of two rectangular rooms connected by a porch, also thatch-roofed, with walls of latticework designed to let air circulate. The compound also contained a menstrual hut. The women worked small garden plots near the family compound, and also contributed labor to large, communal cornfields, whose produce was stored in the village warehouse. The men also worked in the communal gardens.

In the Northeast, by contrast, villages were truly autonomous, in the sense that no higher political authority could compel different villages to cooperate in anything at all. Within the village, which was usually a cluster of large communal dwellings housing clan-related families, there was a council of mature men who deliberated on matters of concern, often in a town meeting where all the men and women could attend, listen, and voice opinion through designated orators. If a consensus was reached, the council could make recommendations on a variety of matters, such as relations with other villages or tribes, a decision to move the village to a new site when the fertility of the cornfields was exhausted, the route to be taken in the winter hunt, the dispatching of ambassadors, attendance at an inter-village "tribal" conclave, or making peace with a group with whom a blood feud had escalated into chronic war.

But these chiefs' recommendations were more advisory than binding. There was rarely a chief who had paramount authority (despite the European conviction that there must be a "king" with whom to do business). The "tribe" was really no more than a group of villages that shared hunting grounds and spoke a common language different from that of adjacent tribes. The tribe thus was rarely an integrated administrative unit and might have no regular council of its own. Tribes speaking related languages often recognized each other as members of an inter-tribal confederacy, but given the amorphous nature of the tribe itself, these confederacies usually had more sentimental than political unity.

In the Northeast, the pinnacle of political integration appears to have been reached by the Iroquois, whose Five Nations (the Mohawks, Oneidas, Onondagas, Cayugas, and Senecas) had shortly before contact with Europeans consolidated their ethnic confederacy into something approaching a federal union of tribes, with a central council of chiefs nominated by women to represent the constituent clans of each tribe. The initial impetus to this union was the recognition of a need to abort blood feuds among the member tribes by persuading aggrieved parties to accept wergild as compensation for their loss in lieu of taking revenge by retaliatory killing. This theme was celebrated in the central ritual of the League of the Iroquois, the Condolence Ceremony, performed on the occasion of the death of a chief. The movement to institute the revitalization of the confederacy was led by a visionary prophet named Hiawatha (whose name was later misappropriated by Longfellow to denominate a legendary Ojibwa hero). Later, however, the league became a vehicle for coordinating Iroquois dealings, military, diplomatic, and economic, with both neighboring tribes and the encroaching Europeans. As a result of the effort by British colonists to use them to influence nearby tribal groups, the Iroquois, who numbered only about fifteen thousand souls, attracted an enor-mous amount of official attention, eclipsing the relatively meager colonial annals of the far more numerous Southeastern Indians.

From the earliest meetings between coastal Indians and Euro-peans, there were exchanges of Native American products— foodstuffs and skins and furs—for European manufactured goods. In time, by the middle of the seventeenth century, this barter grew into an extremely important economic relationship that was then called the "Indian trade" and is now usually referred to as the "fur trade."

The economic importance of the fur trade to the Europeans was immense. The European population was expanding, and skins and furs from America, particularly beaver pelts and deer skins, were highly valued, because local European supplies were running short. Beaver fur was especially prized because it made a superior felt, then in vogue as a material for hats. But furs of other small animals—squirrel, fox, lynx, martin, otter—were also wanted. From the tribes of the Southeast, which did not produce furs of the highest quality, the traders took vast quantities of deer hides. Deerskin in Europe was fashioned into gloves and other articles of leather and was widely used for making the vellum necessary for the bindings of books. The interest of other European manufacturers, however, was equally intense, for merchants who traded with the Indians were a huge new market for iron and steel goods, woolen cloth, clay pipes, glassware, and wampum, and for items of personal decoration, such as glass beads and face paint. For example, the quantities of trade goods imported for sale to the Choctaws in 1750 included more than 5,000 yards of woolen cloth, 1,700 blankets, 2,500 shirts, 150 muskets, 4,000 pounds of gunpowder, 300 pieces of scarlet ribbon, and 43,000 knives. About the same time, the Cherokees were trading some 25,000 deer skins annually.

The Native Americans in the East had made no use of metal in pre-Columbian times, except for copper, hammered into ornaments out of nuggets found in the Great Lakes region. Steel knives, hatchets ("tomahawks"), traps, files, scissors, and other hand tools were quickly taken up to replace less durable, tedious-to-make tools of stone, bone, and wood. Copper pots, pans, and kettles, of course, did not break as easily as native pottery. Woven cloth could be easily tailored into native-style garments. And despite the technical advantages of the bow and arrow for hunting and even warfare, until repeating cartridge-firing rifles became available in the second half of the nineteenth century, the men wanted muskets. Loud, slow to reload, and no more accurate than the bow, they nevertheless were a mark of prestige.

Up to a point, the effect of incorporating these European-made goods was merely one of substituting one item for another, to be used for traditional purposes in an unchanged pattern of culture. Steel axes did the same jobs as stone axes but more efficiently. But a more subtle warping of cultures was soon happening. In order to get sufficient skins and furs to exchange for the newly necessary trade goods, the Indians had to hunt more. Intensive hunting for skins and furs, far beyond what was needed for food and traditional uses of skin, sinew, and bone, inevitably tended to deplete the game. Hunters were forced to forage farther afield, to stay away longer from the home village, perhaps to trespass on other people's hunting grounds, thus inviting violent retaliation. Peltries became, in effect, the equivalent of a cash crop with which to buy indispensable hardware and dry goods.

Furthermore, in order to lubricate the wheels of commerce, unscrupulous traders often sold or gave whiskey to a Native American population that had no experience with any drug more intoxicating than native tobacco or, in the Southeast, the "black drink," a ceremonial emetic. Whether Native Americans were genetically more susceptible to alcoholism is doubtful, but there is no question that the behavioral and physical effects of alcohol ravaged native communities. Indian representatives regularly implored colonial (and, later, federal) authorities to stop the whiskey trade, and sympathetic laws and regulations were promulgated again and again. But the black market in whiskey was never effectively suppressed. Victims of intoxication, male and female, were a familiar sight about the trading posts and even in the villages; deaths and injuries from exposure, accidents, and assault among both the inebriated and their victims were lamentably common. The "drunken Indian" became a popular stereotype of Native Americans, even though contemporary accounts of alcohol abuse among poor urban and frontier whites suggest that alcoholism was as much a white as an Indian problem.

But in addition to game depletion and alcohol abuse, another apocalyptic motif emerged. In the late seventeenth century and the first half of the eighteenth, open conflicts developed among the colonial powers seeking monopoly of the fur trade in various regions. Competition among the various Indian tribes over access to furs and to markets also led to chronic wars, such as the bloody conflicts in the Southeast among rival tribes and between colonial militias and tribal warriors, and the long struggle between the Iroquois of New York and the Indian clients, like the Hurons, of the French in Canada. The wars in the forest led to the virtual extermination of whole tribes along the Atlantic coast, both North and South. The climax was reached with the French and Indian War, in which the British and their Indian allies defeated the French and their Indian allies in North America (and which sparked the worldwide Seven Years' War between Great Britain and France over imperial preeminence). After the close of that war in 1763, Britain seized Canada, and Spain, already occupying Florida, took over the trans-Mississippian territory of Louisiana.

But the wars continued, now over land instead of furs.

The wars over the fur trade substantially ended with the cessation of hostilities between the British and the French in 1763. Later wars were fought primarily about land. For a hundred years previously, the Native Americans had been able to slow down, if not completely prevent, settlement on their territories beyond the coastal plains, by playing off the British, the French, and the Spanish against one another. Up to the end of the French and Indian War, the threat of a tribe's tilting to one side or the other, whether in trade agreements or in military alliances, kept settlers off Indian lands west of a line a hundred miles or so inland, from the St. Lawrence River to the Gulf of Mexico.

In 1763, as part of the settlement of the French and Indian

War, the British crown proclaimed an official boundary for white purchase and settlement within the thirteen colonies. The proclamation was intended to assuage Indian discontent, but it offended many would-be settlers and speculators, and contributed to the resentment that exploded in the American Revolution. The line ran from the Canadian border south through western New England, south across upstate New York through the middle of Iroquois country, and then south along the crest of the Appalachian Mountains through Pennsylvania and the Southern colonies, to Spanish Florida. Most of the province of Georgia (then including what are now the states of Alabama and Mississippi) lay west of the line, preserving intact the lands of the Choctaws and Chickasaws, and taking in only the eastern districts of the Cherokees and Creeks. (A modification of the line in 1768 reserved even more of the Creek and Cherokee lands in Georgia to their Native American owners, but opened up Kentucky and eastern Tennessee to purchase and settlement by whites.) At the same time, British troops were establishing garrisons in some of the old French forts west of the line, and new regulations were imposed on the fur trade, limiting credit to the hunters and reducing the prices paid for furs, and virtually ending the traditional practice of presenting large quantities of goods as "gifts" at every conference.

The consequence of garrisoning British troops in the French forts was an uprising of the Northern tribes. Generally known as the "Conspiracy of Pontiac," it was actually the first effort at a pan-Indian political and military alliance. The inspiration for this movement was a Delaware prophet named Neolin. Neolin had a vision in which he met the Master of Life, who told him that the Indians must drive the British soldiers out of the Indian country and must give up their addiction to alcohol and their dependence on European trade goods. The prophet's message influenced primarily the tribes of the Great Lakes region and the Ohio Valley. When Pontiac laid siege to Detroit in May of 1763, nearly simultaneous attacks were launched against other British forts from Niagara west to Illinois. More than half a dozen British posts were captured, but Detroit held out and the siege was lifted after five months. Within a year British troops recaptured the other outposts and the war was over.

The Southern tribes took no part in the uprising of 1763. The Cherokees had lost thousands of warriors fighting against the British in the French and Indian War, and the other tribes had also suffered from backing the French. Now fearing reprisals, the Cherokees in a series of treaties from 1763 to 1765 ceded most of their lands east of the proclamation line.

Although some tribes and factions joined the colonists during the American Revolution (1776–83), many turned against them. To the north, most of the Iroquois joined the British, ravaging frontier settlements in a wide arc from the Mohawk Valley in New York, across central Pennsylvania, to the borders of Maryland. Shawnees and Delawares attacked in the Ohio Valley. And in the South, the Cherokees once again waged war on the frontiers in Georgia, North and South Carolina, and Virginia. Colonial forces in response made punitive, scorched-earth raids into Indian country, North and South, burning Cherokee and Iroquois villages and cornfields, leaving many survivors to die of starvation and disease. A legacy of bitterness over atrocities on both sides remained for generations, Western frontiersmen condemning the Indians as murdering savages and Indians despising the Americans as untrustworthy and brutal.

The peace agreement between Great Britain and the colonial confederation in 1783 did not mention the Indians. Between 1784 and 1789, various American authorities (not all of them federal) and various, usually unaccredited, "chiefs" of one tribe after another signed peace treaties that included large land cessions in both the North and the South. Claiming that these were legal cessions of land, particularly in the Northeast, the Congress in 1787 enacted the Northwest Ordinance, which proposed to organize a government for the supposedly ceded area north of the Ohio River and east of the Mississippi. Short of cash to pay back wages to the soldiers of the Revolution and to meet other financial obligations, the government hoped to pay off the veterans with land grants in Ohio, and to sell off other public lands to hungrily waiting land companies.

More war ensued. In the South, the Creeks and the Cherokees took up arms against the United States as early as 1786; a peace settlement was not achieved until 1795. But as usual, from the beginning of the colonial period, most of the new nation's attention was focused on the Northern tribes, and particularly on the Iroquois and their allies in the Ohio country, exposed as they were to the suspected machinations of the British in Canada. In the Northwest Territory, the tribes condemned the postwar land cessions as fraudulent, and as Joseph Brant, the Iroquois leader, had urged, formed a confederation to resist American encroachment. After desultory border warfare, large-scale military action began. In 1790, an army of militia was crushed by the Indians in the forests of the Maumee Valley in Ohio. In 1791 a confederate Indian force destroyed the major part of the U.S. regular army under the command of General Arthur St. Clair on the upper Wabash River in Indiana; the defeat cost the Americans 630 dead and 300 wounded out of a force of 1,400 men. But in 1794 a better-organized expedition, led by General "Mad Anthony" Wayne, finally defeated the confederate warriors in Ohio at the Battle of Fallen Timbers. At the Treaty of Greenville the next year, the Indian tribes ceded much of Ohio to the United States but retained a large part of the territory that had been lost in the earlier, fraudulent, treaties. And—of great significance for Indian land claims in the twentieth century—the Treaty of Greenville contained language that implied that a guardian-and-ward relationship would henceforth obtain between the government of the United States and the Indian tribes within its territory. In effect, the United States government assumed responsibility for ensuring that Native Americans would be dealt with fairly and honorably in the future, including future treaties to arrange cessions of land.

But there was to be one more effort to create a pan-Indian confederation and to drive out the encroaching whites, and this one was embraced by tribes in the South as well as the North.

Another religious prophet, Tenskwatawa, the "Shawnee prophet," and his part-Creek brother Tecumseh preached resistance. The prophet was able to unite the Ohio tribes under his brother's leadership, and in 1811 Tecumseh himself traveled South, attempting to persuade the Southern tribes to join the union. Tecumseh's mother was Creek and he was able to convert a large number of Creeks—the "Red Sticks"—to his cause. ("Red Sticks" was the traditional Creek designation for the war chiefs and the red pole they erected in the villages as a signal to mobilize for war.) But he was unable to bring all the Southern tribes into the larger confederacy that he envisaged. While Tecumseh was away, the prophet attacked a camp of American soldiers led by William Henry Harrison, the governor of Indiana Territory. In the subsequent battle of Tippecanoe, the Indians were defeated and the prophet's village was destroyed.

When the War of 1812 between England and the United States began, Tecumseh's warriors sided with the British. But the British and Indian forces in the Great Lakes area were beaten in battle and Tecumseh was killed. In the South, the Creek nativist faction, the Red Sticks, also sided with the British and attacked and destroyed a fort and settlement, Fort Mims, in what is now Mississippi, and massacred some four hundred whites of all ages and both sexes. In response, in 1814 General Andrew Jackson, commander of the Tennessee militia, marched into the Creek country and eventually in a major battle at the Horseshoe Bend of the Tallapoosa River in Alabama defeated the Red Sticks (with the help of Cherokee warriors), with heavy losses to the Creeks. A few months after the battle, at the treaty of Fort Jackson in August 1814, Jackson forced the Creeks to cede most of their land in Georgia and Alabama. He then went on in 1815 to national fame by successfully defending New Orleans from British attack (again with the help of Indian warriors).

With the death of Tecumseh, effective resistance by the Northeastern Indians to white territorial expansion had largely come to an end. But major resistance continued in the South, most of it by peaceful means, with the conspicuous exception of the Seminole Wars in Florida, which began in 1817 and dragged on for twenty-five years. During that period, national attention in Indian affairs would focus on the Cherokees, Creeks, Choctaws, Chickasaws, and Seminoles of the Southeast, soon to be known as the Five Civilized Tribes because of their successful adoption of many white customs.

2

THE CONFLICT OVER

FEDERAL INDIAN POLICY

THE original colonies from Maine to South Carolina had been largely abandoned by their Native American populations well before the Revolution, except for western Pennsylvania and New York. Georgia alone supported a massive Indian population. Small reservations of a few thousand acres had been set up in the seventeenth and eighteenth centuries in the New England provinces and southward, and here and there small off-reservation "remnant groups" survived, of uncertain origin and racial mixture. All these little reservations and enclaves were legally subject to colonial jurisdiction, but the management of local affairs was usually left to the Indian residents, and colonial officials acted more as guardians than as supervisors.

Over the years, many of the reservations were whittled away and sold, but in 1830 there still remained a number: several thousand Iroquois in New York State, over two thousand souls on several reserves in New England, a few hundred on small reserves in Virginia, and several hundred more in the Carolinas. These small groups were no threat, economic or military, to the surrounding white settlements and were not under any great pressure to move away. The major issue that remained, up to the passage of the Removal Act in 1830, was the much larger Native American presence in Georgia, Alabama, Mississippi, and Florida, where Indians still occupied most of the agricultural land.

*   *   *

The earliest efforts to formulate a federal Indian policy were focused on the Northeast, and some important precedents set there were applied later to the Indian population of the Deep South.

After the Revolution, there was intense pressure to acquire Indian land, by debt-ridden states and a federal government anxious to use public land to pay off war debts, and from speculators who saw fortunes to be made from the sale of thousands of square miles of virgin timber and agricultural acreage, of waterways, mill sites, harbors, and so forth. Between 1786 and 1788, private land companies operating under state charters bought up the Iroquois lands east of the Genesee River, and most of the remaining tract between the Genesee and Lake Erie was sold by the Senecas in 1797 to the Netherlands-based Holland Land Company. The Senecas, however, retained several substantial reservations, which the company (and its successor, the British-owned Ogden Land Company) held an option to purchase. As we shall see later, the Ogden Land Company's dispute with the Senecas became a national *cause célèbre* in the 1830s and '40s in the aftermath of the passage of the Removal Act.

The United States itself was merely an observer in the Iroquois purchases, but it had its own agenda: to acquire the land in what is now northeastern Ohio. Part of that land would be donated to veterans of the Revolution in lieu of back pay; part would be sold off to land companies and private speculators. Under the theory that the United States had conquered the Indians in the Revolutionary War and therefore already held title to the land, the U.S. commissioners at the Treaties of Fort Stanwix, Fort McIntosh, and Fort Finney in 1784, 1785, and 1786 "gave" peace to the Iroquois and the Indians of Ohio. In return, the Indians present at these meetings promised that their tribes would vacate much of their land north of the Ohio River and restrict themselves to reservations within the area ceded. The response to these proceedings by the Ohio tribes was outrage. They denounced the treaties as fraudulent and invalid, attended by unauthorized individuals who did not represent the tribes and who allowed themselves to be threatened, bribed, and plied with liquor until they signed away their own and their neighbors' birthright. An intertribal Western Confederacy was formed to prevent survey and settlement, and an ugly border warfare developed between frontiersmen attempting to enter Indian territory and warriors determined to drive them back.

Realizing that reliance on a claim of conquest would merely result in a long, bloody, and expensive war, Congress backed away from that position. In the Northwest Ordinance of 1787, designed to organize the new territory once peace was restored, it was explicitly stated that Indian "land and property shall never be taken from them without their consent." Recognizing that the earlier treaties would have to be renegotiated, a conference for that purpose was held at Fort Harmar in Ohio in 1789. The few Indians who showed up confirmed the earlier cessions, but their actions were repudiated by the confederacy. Even white observers were disgusted by these disgraceful proceedings in which only a few, unrepresentative Indians participated and no interpreter could be found who spoke English.

Although the Treaty of Fort Harmar was also rejected by the Indians, it and the Northwest Ordinance had a major significance nonetheless: they demonstrated that the United States had abandoned the conquest theory and now explicitly recognized the principle that the Native Americans had a right to their land. Just after the treaty, Henry Knox, the Secretary of War, wrote a letter to President Washington formally expressing this new policy, which became the basis for subsequent purchases of land from the Indians. Knox advised Washington not to claim a U.S. right to the soil based on a theory of conquest or implied cession from Great Britain, or to insist on the corollary right to expel the Indians from their lands without payment. The Indian tribes should be considered as foreign nations. The United States, and any individual state, had only a preemption right—an exclusive option—to purchase Indian land. The new policy (which was actually a return to former British colonial practice) was quickly implemented by the passage in 1790 of an act regulating Indian trade and land purchases. This act required that all sales of land by Indians, whether to the United States or to persons, companies, or states having a preemption right derived from earlier colonial authority or from the United States, must be made at a public treaty held under the authority of the United States.

Despite the enunciation of this new policy, however, the Western Confederacy was not satisfied, and plans for a grand peace conference in 1793 had to be abandoned when the tribes refused to send delegates. As we described in the last chapter, open warfare between the confederacy and the United States began in 1790 and continued until the Indians and the United States made peace by the Treaty of Greenville in 1795. In addition to the importance of the peace agreement and of the corollary major cession of land in eastern and southern Ohio, Greenville again articulated the philosophy and rhetoric of a protective federal relationship with Indian tribes.

Thus, from 1795 on, a federal Indian policy was in place that defined the tribes of Native Americans (in the words later used by Chief Justice Marshall of the Supreme Court) as "domestic dependent nations," owning and occupying their land, and sufficiently sovereign for the federal government to deal with them by treaty, but enjoying only an uncertain degree of self-governance. It was the ambiguity of the right of Native Americans to local self-government that would prove to be the chink in the armor of federal protection.

The statesmen who made Indian policy during the early federal period were advocates of "Indian reform" (and some of them of Indian removal as well). Philosophical gentlemen well versed in the values of the Enlightenment, they saw the Native Americans not as an inferior species (as some of their compatriots thought) but as untutored natural men, possessed of reason and capable of learning both the best and the worst habits of civilized Europeans. The temporary 1790 Intercourse Act and the subsequent Intercourse Act of 1802, and even the revised Intercourse Act of 1834, sought to prevent exploitation and corruption of the Indians by vicious and unscrupulous traders by means of a strict system of licenses, and they provided severe penalties for unauthorized intrusions upon Indian land. The Act of 1802 also called for an appropriation of $15,000 (later reduced to $10,000) annually as an education fund, to be used to provide agents who would reside among the Indians and to supply "useful domestic animals and implements of husbandry." In 1806, another piece of legislation established a government factory system under the direction of a Superintendent of Indian Trade that would (until it was abolished in 1822) compete with private traders.

With the end of the War of 1812, the nation entered a period of peace and economic development. The technology of the Industrial Revolution began to appear in the Northeastern states. American writers and artists flourished. And a widespread movement of social reform, led in part by ecumenical, low-church Protestants of several denominations, sought to save the souls and to improve the manners and morals of all white Americans. The movement proposed to eliminate drunkenness, prostitution, illiteracy, and of course "infidelity" (i.e., failure to adhere to Christianity) in all social classes. The most enthusiastically evangelical wing of the movement, indeed, aimed at no less than bringing all the heathens of the world to Christ. Universal salvation was their goal and the "foreign" mission was their instrument. The Native Americans were considered to be heathens and therefore as legitimate an object of missionary effort as Hindus, Mohammedans, and pagan South Sea islanders.

Attempts to convert the Native Americans to Christianity had been in vogue since the seventeenth century, when the celebrated Jesuit missions to the Iroquois were launched and Protestants in New England evangelized Algonkian tribes. In addition to preaching in the native languages, missionaries often tried to educate and "civilize" selected youths, at stations like the Indian Charity School at Lebanon, Connecticut, presided over by Eleazar Wheelock (later the founder of Dartmouth College). Efforts to convert and educate the more accessible Eastern Iroquois—the Mohawks and the Oneidas—had produced some small Christian congregations and at least one spectacularly successful Indian leader, Joseph Brant. The celebrated Jonathan Edwards and his pupil David Brainerd had made converts of Mahicans and Delawares during the Great Awakening of the 1740s.

But these somewhat spasmodic efforts were supplanted in the latter half of the eighteenth century by the more systematic approaches of the Unitas Fratrum (the Moravians) and the Society of Friends (the Quakers). From the 1740s until well into the nineteenth century, the Moravians maintained missions among the Delaware Indians of Pennsylvania, and followed them in their migrations westward, eventually to new homes in Canada and west of the Mississippi. Other Moravian missionaries worked among the Southern Indians. Wherever possible, the Moravians set up small planned religious communities, led by white missionaries and by native converts. In addition to providing havens for converts, these communities were also, in effect, technical schools that trained Indians in the use of the tools and equipment necessary to farm in the European manner. Similarly, late in the eighteenth century, Quaker meetings in Philadelphia and Baltimore sent Quaker families to live among the Senecas and other Indian groups; they imported heavy equipment such as sawmill irons and blacksmith's and wheelwright's tools, and set up demonstration farms to teach the men to plow and care for livestock and the women to sew, spin, and make soap.

The congregations back home whose donations supported these efforts received encouraging reports of progress. They firmly believed the Indians to be just as capable of living industrious, peaceable Christian lives as the rest of humanity. Thus, when the era of reform unfolded in the 1820s, there was a sizable public ready to perceive Native Americans not as violent, wandering hunters and warriors but as men and women capable of religious salvation and advancement to the exalted level of Christian civilization. The forest romances of James Fenimore Cooper, whose novels *The Pioneers* (1823) and *The Last of the Mohicans* (1826) featured Indians with moral qualities that whites could admire, contributed to the positive image. And the Moravian missionary John Heckewelder's *History, Manners, and Customs of the Indian Nations* (1818), an account chiefly of his own beloved Delawares, set a tone of sympathy for aboriginal culture and of optimism about Indian improvement that helped to give legitimacy to cries for renewed effort to promote the assimilation of the Indians into the mainstream of American society.

The Native American policy of accommodation to the presence of the whites that followed the end of the forest wars in the 1790s thus met an enthusiastic response from the reform movement's religious constituency. This constituency had many representatives in Congress and the administration, and was able to flood Congress with hundreds of petitions in support of an "Indian reform" or "civilization" policy. In addition to the establishment of more mission schools among the Indians, another goal of the benevolent associations was the restriction or elimination of the whiskey trade, that black market in alcohol that had long devastated Indian communities. Here the role of the federal Superintendent of Indian Trade was crucial. The federal factory system was directly under the control of this official, and for years, from 1806 until it was abolished in 1822, it was able to carry on a substantial commerce with the Indians without selling liquor. But private traders, both Indian and white, defied government regulation and continued to import liquor into the Indian country.

Indian reform obviously could best be accomplished among a people securely settled on their own land and near enough to the Eastern centers of benevolence to be readily accessible to missionaries. The goal of Indian reform thus did not include removal. The movement for Indian reform was, however, in conflict with a covert government agenda to persuade the Eastern Indians to sell their lands and emigrate west of the Mississippi.

The believers in the possibility of Indian reform in situ were largely concentrated in the industrial and commercial centers of the Northeast, far from the Southern and Western states where most of the Indians lived. But from northern Michigan Territory, down across the Middle West, and into the Deep South, there existed a rural and small-town white population that had borne the brunt of the Indian wars, from the beginning of the French and Indian War in 1755 to the end of the Creek War in 1814. During these wars thousands of white families had lost members, in battle or in raids on farms and frontier settlements; hundreds survived with wounds; hundreds more had fled, to find when they returned that their farms had been burned and their livestock driven away or slaughtered; thousands more knew relatives, friends, and neighbors who had suffered similar losses. And others read of death, destruction, and torture in the popular "captivity" narratives that told harrowing tales of children abducted during attacks that killed their parents. It did not matter that whites had inflicted far greater casualties on Native Americans. In the 1820s, a mere decade after the last major Indian war, the Indians were still regarded as a menace, not merely on account of their own military potential, but because many of the Northern tribes retained close ties to Great Britain, the national enemy still occupying Canada, and many of the Southern tribes held friendly communication with various administrations in Mexico (which then included Texas) and Spanish Florida. To be sure, President Monroe had announced his famous "Monroe Doctrine" in 1823, notifying European powers not to interfere in the internal affairs of the nations of the Western Hemisphere. But the very need to promulgate such a doctrine merely reinforced the perception that Great Britain and Spain might,

with Indian help, attempt to reestablish their old colonial hege-
monies.

Settlers on the frontiers regarded Indians as dangerous
neighbors. The best course of action would be to drive them
off, or exterminate them, and seize their lands for use by
virtuous, God-fearing white farmers. These settlers were a
constituency ready-made to support politicians who proposed a
drastic solution to the Indian problem—wholesale removal.

As we noted earlier, most of the country's leaders in Congress,
the White House, and the federal courts were, however, not
redneck frontiersmen. They tended to be well-educated men of
the world, schooled in the professions, particularly law, and
possessed of ample personal means. At least after the abandon-
ment of the conquest theory, they were, for the most part,
disposed to be guided by the traditional British concept of
colonial sovereignty as it applied to indigenous native populations. With this concept, the sovereign power—whether mon-
archy or republic—recognized that aboriginal peoples had a
right to continue in the use of the land they occupied. The
sovereign power, in this case the United States, held an exclusive
option to buy that carried with it the obligation to obtain the
consent of the natives to any purchase of their land and to pay
fair compensation. But it was also deemed a principle of natural
law, as expressed by such philosophers as Emmerich de Vattel,
whose widely read book, *The Law of Nations* (1758), asserted that
the right of the agriculturist to acquire land for expansion was
superior to the claim of the primitive hunter. Vattel's views, and
those of other Enlightenment philosophers, on the rights of
man had also given inspiration to Americans seeking freedom
from Britain.

A federal removal policy was adumbrated as early as 1783,
when George Washington (an old Indian fighter), while com-
paring the Indian to the wolf as "both being beasts of prey,"
declared that the "gradual extension of our settlements will as
certainly cause the savage, as the wolf, to retire . . ." Thomas
Jefferson was far more sympathetic to the Native Americans,

but in a pitying way that boded ill for their future. He considered Indians to be the intellectual equals of whites. He was much interested in Indian languages and antiquities and promoted Indian research by scholars at the American Philosophical Society in Philadelphia, of which he was president. He held out the possibility that Indians might in due course take up white farming methods and "incorporate with us as citizens of the United States." But he really wanted them to remove beyond the Mississippi. After the Louisiana Purchase in 1803, he actively sought the passage of a constitutional amendment to provide, among other things, for the transporting of the Eastern Indians to the newly acquired territory. He personally solicited the Chickasaws to sell their land and move West. And he even went so far as to advocate chicanery in order to separate the natives from their lands, suggesting that traders might see to it that "the good and influential individuals run in debt" because, once inextricably entangled, they would be willing to pay the debt "by a cession of lands."

By the 1820s, the term "colonization" had become a popular label for the concept of solving social problems by the physical removal of undesirables. One of many so-called benevolent associations, the American Colonization Society, was dedicated to the repatriation of black freedmen to West Africa (the colony founded there in 1820 eventually became the nation of Liberia). President Monroe even assigned naval vessels to escort the ships carrying the black colonists. And now, when the policy of civilizing and assimilating the Indians was accused of being a failure, if not a mistake to begin with, the idea of colonizing the Indians west of the Mississippi gained favor.

President Monroe in his message to Congress in 1820 recommended legislation to encourage voluntary removal, and his Secretary of War, John C. Calhoun, earnestly supported such a project. In 1824, Monroe again asked Congress to enact removal legislation. But no removal bill was passed during Monroe's term in office.

Monroe was succeeded by John Quincy Adams. In 1825, at

the outset of Adams's presidency, his Secretary of War, James Barbour, sent a proposal for a removal bill to the House Committee on Indian Affairs that envisioned one great Indian territory west of the Mississippi with a territorial government "maintained by the United States" (perhaps implying future admission into the Union as a state). The plan was to invite decisions to remove by individual Indians rather than by tribes and to encourage an eventual amalgamation of all the tribes into "one mass," with property to be distributed among the individuals. Such a bill, however, was not introduced.

Toward the end of his term, Adams contemplated a reorganization of the administration of Indian affairs. Lewis Cass of Michigan and William Clark of Missouri, the two regional superintendents under Thomas McKenney, head of the Indian Office, were called to Washington to work with McKenney in preparing a report on the regulation of trade and intercourse with the Indians. Although the report did not explicitly deal with the subject of removal, concerning itself rather with trade, annuities, and the bureaucracy of the Office of Indian Affairs and its dozens of local agencies, it rather delicately suggested the inevitability of removal, observing that "some of the tribes evidently occupy positions where they cannot expect long to remain."

One Southern legislator even offered a compromise scheme. Senator John Forsyth of Georgia in 1823 proposed the establishment of one giant reservation, *east* of the Mississippi, on which would be concentrated members of all the tribes. Land would be allotted to each family, not alienable until the year 1900, when all would become citizens of the United States. The government of the district would be in the hands of Congress, but the Indians would elect their own local assembly (a system perhaps modeled after the District of Columbia). Indians not willing to submit to these regulations were to be removed beyond the Mississippi. But although Forsyth was convinced that his plan would confer "important benefits on this hapless race," he was also convinced that it was unconstitutional, because it infringed upon the rights of the states, and he never presented the contemplated bill to Congress.

And so Congress did not take up the challenge. The moral issue was still moot. There were, in fact, two federal administrative policies at work side by side, a policy of "Indian reform" and a policy of "removal." It was left to an educated frontiersman, Lewis Cass, the governor and Superintendent of Indian Affairs of the Michigan Territory, to formulate a politically acceptable rationale for implementing a policy of removal.

Lewis Cass (1782–1866) was an early authority on the American Indian whose views gave intellectual respectability to the political position of Andrew Jackson on removal. His most recent biographer asserts that in his day, up to the mid-1830s, he was "the foremost authority in the United States on the languages and cultures of the northern tribes." As ex-officio Superintendent of Indian Affairs for the Michigan Territory, of which he was governor from 1813 to 1831, he was in frequent personal contact with the Indian peoples of the Ohio Valley and the upper Great Lakes. From the agents whom he appointed from time to time to deal with the various tribes, he systematically collected answers to a printed questionnaire that he prepared, inquiring about Indian languages, behavior, and beliefs. He wrote influential articles on Indian matters in the highly respected *North American Review* and was elected to membership in the American Philosophical Society in 1826 in recognition of his "considerable knowledge of the habits, manners, customs, and languages of the Aborigenes of this Country . . . He has collected ample materials of information on these subjects, which he is preparing for publication." Although Cass never published his major work on the Indians, grateful twentieth-century anthropologists have used some of the surviving responses to his questionnaire in ethnohistorical research.

Historians know a somewhat different Lewis Cass. In 1831, President Andrew Jackson appointed Cass Secretary of War, and he remained on the Washington scene as a Democratic politician for the rest of his life. As Secretary of War from 1831 to 1836, Cass was responsible, among other things, for the management of Indian affairs, and in that capacity he arranged for land cessions and supervised the removal of most of the Eastern tribes in accordance with the terms of the Indian Removal Act of 1830. He prosecuted the Black Hawk War in 1832 and the Second Seminole War from 1832 to 1836. He went on to a long and distinguished career as minister to France (1836–42), senator from Michigan (1845–57), candidate for President (1848), and Secretary of State (1857–60).

Although Cass's role in national politics was very important, perhaps his most enduring impact on the country was achieved during his eighteen years as governor of the Michigan Territory. During that time he expounded a set of ideas about the Indians that rationalized the popular demand for the removal of all the Native Americans in the East to new homes west of the Mississippi. By 1830, he was arguing that Indian removal was not only legally, economically, and morally justified but was also morally necessary, because only by emigration could the Native Americans survive as a race and become civilized. Cass's ideas were not original with him, especially the self-serving belief that savage Indian hunters must give up their vast hunting grounds to more productive agriculturists, a doctrine, as we have seen, long put forth by European philosophers of natural law. But Cass's extensive practical knowledge of the tribes of the Northeast, and to a lesser extent of the South, and his ability to write clear and forceful prose that brought together social and ethnographic data with legalistic argument, gave him an intellectual influence both on political policy and on the course of ethnological theory.

Cass had a particular interest in Indian languages. The version of the questionnaire that he published in 1823, for instance, devoted forty-four of its sixty-four pages to Indian languages, including a long discussion of his notions about phonetic transcription and grammatical analysis, using Latin conjugations and declensions as a model. He took the view that the style of a language constrains and reveals the thought processes of its speakers, and he claimed that the American aborigines were, because of peculiarities in their languages, unable to distinguish the abstract from the concrete and thus were incapable of logical reasoning. Cass was not a racist in the ordinary sense of the word, however: he depicted the Indians not as constitutionally but as linguistically inferior to Europeans, resting on a lower rung of the universal ladder of cultural progress; but his doctrine served to rationalize highly discriminatory governmental policies.

Equally important in Cass's thought was the concept of the "hunter state." The hunter state was a stage in the progress of mankind toward civilization, a stage through which Europeans had long since passed. The Indians of Eastern North America, both in the North and in the South, he believed, still remained in the hunter state. But Cass recognized that recently there had been changes in the condition of these hunters—changes for the worse. When Europeans first arrived, they found a savage but stable society, in which the Native American men could indulge their twin passions, for hunting and for war, without restraint. Then the Europeans began to trade for skins and furs, giving the Indians in return not only useful trade goods but also whiskey, the Indians' curse. The need for extra peltries to pay for trade goods and whiskey led to overhunting and the depletion of game. The result, he asserted, was increased intertribal warfare, bloody conflict with settlers, involvement in wars among the Europeans, and the sale of land. Eventually confined to reservations, the Indians entered a third phase of the hunter state, a degenerate condition of squalid poverty, marked by drunkenness, murder and mayhem, disease, and general corruption by vices introduced by unscrupulous whiskey traders and squatters. It was this last phase that Cass saw most vividly around him and that contrasted so starkly with the optimistic observations offered by advocates of Indian reform.

Cass's analysis of the ill effects of the trade culture and the Indian wars was correct enough. But Cass paid scant attention to one major fact: throughout the area occupied by the Eastern Indians, *horticulture*, not hunting, actually provided the staple foods of the native diet—corn, squash, and beans—and fish and shellfish were as important as venison in supplying protein. In this, as we now know, the Eastern Indians were typical of horticultural or "neolithic"-level communities around the world. And it may be noted that even traditional hunters and gatherers in temperate and tropical climates commonly secure the bulk of their calories from wild vegetable products, fish, and shellfish. Nor did Cass pay much attention to the fact that this horticultural economy was carried on in the Northeast, both in pre-Columbian times and after, exclusively by women, and by both women and men in the Southeast. What Indian men should do, he declared, was learn to plow and keep domestic animals, and the women should spin, weave, and make soap—just as the Indian reformers wanted them to do. But the men would not undertake this new role, because they were incapable of reason (their language was defective) and they were irredeemably attached to the pleasures of the chase and the warpath. Nor did Cass think that Whiggish do-gooders would soon be able to civilize them, despite a few local successes.

At times, Cass's rhetoric in presenting this thesis became vituperative. In an article in the *North American Review* (1827) entitled "Service of Indians in Civilized Warfare," he bitterly criticized the British for employing savage warriors during the American Revolution and the War of 1812. He accused the Indians of slaughtering men, women, and children "with circumstances of atrocity, to which no parallel can be found in other ages or nations." Much of this rhetoric may be interpreted, however, mainly as criticism of British policy, for General Cass was an old soldier, a veteran of the unsuccessful American invasion of Canada during the War of 1812, and a perennial opponent of the imperial British presence in Canada, which he saw as imperiling the American border and which called for unceasing vigilance in defense of American liberty. British criticism of American mistreatment of the Indians was particularly galling to him. In contrast to British practice in Canada, the policy of the United States toward its Indian neighbors, he argued, was singularly benevolent.

But that "benevolence" did not mean that the Indians should be suffered to retain hunting grounds that whites needed for agricultural and commercial settlement. In two articles in the *North American Review*—the 1827 piece just cited and an 1830 essay entitled "Removal of the Indians"—his language was flamboyantly negative. He disclaimed belief "in that system of legal metaphysics, which would give to a few naked and wandering savages, a perpetual title to an immense continent." He saw no capacity for progress in the Indian character: "A principle of progressive improvement seems almost inherent in human nature . . . But there is little of all this in the constitution of our savages." He described their present condition as one of "want and imbecility." He defended American policy, nonetheless. British commentators might falsely claim that the United States policy was that "the Indians shall be made to vanish before civilization, as the snow melts before the sunbeam." To the contrary, Cass asserted, Americans had made it their national policy, as Thomas Jefferson put it, "to extend their care and patronage over the Indian tribes within their limits."

Cass was extremely disparaging of writers who found much of value in Indian character. For John Dunn Hunter, who in 1823 published a memoir of his captivity among the Kickapoo and Osage Indians, he had only contempt and criticism. He called him "one of the boldest" of literary impostors; Hunter's book, he asserted, was a "worthless fabrication . . . beneath the dignity of criticism." He attempted to expose Hunter's ignorance of the history and customs of the Indians with whom he claimed to have lived by reciting allegedly contradictory ethnographic and historical evidence, and he produced letters from persons in the Missouri region, some of whom Hunter claimed to have known, who denied ever having met or heard of him. Modern scholarship, however, has shown that it was Cass, not Hunter, who was in error on some of the particulars. And part of Cass's ire derived from the fact that Hunter's book had been favorably reviewed in the *London Quarterly Review*, and Hunter himself on a visit to England had been warmly received by a number of distinguished persons, including utopian socialist Robert Owen. Hunter actually became a follower of Owen and later was murdered while attempting to establish a utopian community of Indians in Texas.

Cass was not much more charitable toward the old Moravian missionary John Heckewelder, whose book about the Delawares he compared unfavorably with his subagent Henry R. Schoolcraft's account of travels among the Indians of the upper Mississippi Valley. Heckewelder wrote sympathetically about his former charges and sought to convey a sense of their view of the world and its history; he recorded Delaware legends as they were told to him, without attempting to verify their historical accuracy. Cass found this practice unacceptable. Although, as he said, Heckewelder was a kindly and venerable man, he was suffering from "enfeebled faculties" when he wrote his book. "His account," said Cass, "is a pure, unmixed panegyric," composed by one who enjoyed "a spirit of credulity . . . utterly irreconcilable with the cautious deliberation of an historian." Cass deplored the influence upon popular literature of this kind of unrealistic, as he saw it, appreciation of the Indians, and he noted with disdain James Fenimore Cooper's use of Heckewelder's images. He then went on for twenty-eight pages to criticize Heckewelder's supposed misunderstanding of the Delaware language (which Heckewelder spoke and Cass did not).

Cass's animus against the Reverend Mr. Heckewelder must be understood as a function of partisan politics. By and large, evangelical Protestant clergymen, who supported "foreign missions" all over the world, believed that the aborigines of America were worthy and capable of salvation and civilization. But this same evangelical movement was Whiggish in politics, anti-

Masonic (Cass was a Mason and the first master of the Grand Lodge of Michigan), supportive of Henry Clay, generally in favor of free soil, the emancipation of blacks, and a protective tariff for American industry. For the most part, the evangelicals were less jingoistic and expansionist than the Democrats. Favorable depictions of Indian character and mental abilities were thus seen by Cass as part and parcel of a Whiggish, pro-British plot to block America's westward expansion.

In his writings in 1827 Cass did not come out in favor of wholesale removal, which he regarded as a scheme "both controversial and intolerably difficult and expensive" (as indeed it proved to be). But in 1830, in his article "Removal of the Indians," he took a different view, applauding the plan soon to be proposed by President Jackson for the emigration of the Eastern Indians to new hunting grounds west of the Mississippi. Force and bribery, of course, should not be used; persuasion would suffice to make them leave. Nothing less could prevent the further degradation, impoverishment, and eventual demise of these "wandering barbarians."

To some extent Cass was correct in his characterization of the Eastern Indians. Many of the smaller communities, particularly in the North, were slums in the wilderness, occupied by demoralized hunters unable to hunt, warriors unable to fight, riddled by disease, many addicted to alcohol; men, women, and children alike were all too often the victims of mutual mayhem and murder; and their chiefs were notoriously open to bribery by whites seeking to buy land or acquire other privileges. These realities indeed did not appear in the more sentimental literature about Indians. But nonetheless, Cass's theory of the degeneracy of the remnants of the hunter state seriously misrepresented the actual condition, which I shall describe in the next chapter, of some of the Native American communities east of the Mississippi River. In the Northeast, with which Cass was most familiar, he should have known about the remarkable cultural transformation that had taken place among the Senecas and other

Iroquois Indians of New York State. And he should also have known, as one who claimed to be an authority on all Indians, not only of the impressive recent progress of the Five Civilized Tribes of the Southeast but also of their traditional practice of communal agriculture and their large, well-planned towns.

The arrogant disregard by Cass and his contemporaries of Native American agriculture, organized around permanent settlements, may in part have been caused by a kind of gender bias. To Cass and many others, what constituted a people's character, their economic system, their political structure, was what the *men* did. Women's economic and political contribution was auxiliary, of secondary importance; women cooked, made garments, bore and raised children—and maybe puttered about in their little gardens in their spare time. To Cass, the central fact was that the men "wandered about" on their tribal hunting grounds, during the fall and winter securing food for their families, and in the summer prowling the forests as ruthless warriors.

Thus, in his view "they" (i.e., the men) were ill adapted to sedentary civilized life and languished in indolence and vice when unable any longer to hunt and fight. The only solution was to remove the Indians to the forests and plains west of the Mississippi, where they could choose either to return to their former way of life in the untrammeled hunter state or to gradually embrace civilization.

Thus, when Jackson took office as President, there existed a deep division in the nation regarding the proper Indian policy of the states and the federal government, a division between advocates of "civilizing" the Native Americans in the communities where they now lived east of the Mississippi and proponents of removing them to an Indian territory west of the Mississippi, where they could choose the path to civilization if they wished, or continue to follow their traditional way of life. The government for decades had maintained a dual policy, on the one hand appropriating money for educational purposes and trying to improve living conditions on their present reserves, while at the same time urging them to sell their lands and move westward, out of the way of white settlements.

Jackson and his cohorts were determined to shift federal policy toward final and irrevocable removal.

3

THE REMOVAL ACT

A FTER his victory over the Creeks at the Battle of Horseshoe Bend in 1814, Andrew Jackson was appointed major general in the regular army. This position, and the national attention he had earned for defeating the British in the defense of New Orleans, gave him sudden influence in Washington. As I noted in the Introduction, he used that influence to secure appointment as commissioner at a series of treaties with the Southern Indians from 1814 to 1820. He so dominated the treaty proceedings and their aftermath that it can be said that he almost single-handedly established a de facto removal policy that was endorsed by Presidents Monroe and Adams, and was finally enacted into law after Jackson himself became President. In view of their importance in setting policy precedents, it is necessary to review these treaties in some detail.

The Treaty of Fort Jackson in 1814, in which the general exacted from the hungry and dispirited Creeks the cession of about 23 million acres, embracing most of the future state of Alabama and a large part of southern Georgia, started the process. No reputable chiefs were present from the Upper Creek towns, which had supplied most of the hostile forces; their chiefs and many of their warriors and families, including the later-famous Osceola, had fled south to Florida to join other Creek refugees there, known as Seminoles. Lower Creek chiefs, who for the most part had remained at peace during the war, signed away not only most of the Upper Creek territory to the north and west but also a substantial portion of their own lands in southern Georgia.

The northern limit of the cession was left vaguely defined as the Cherokee-Creek boundary. Cherokee ownership of lands in Georgia south of the Tennessee River, acquired as a result of successive wars against the Creeks, had been acknowledged by the United States in the Hopewell Treaty of 1785 and again confirmed in 1806. Chickasaw rights to some lands south of the Tennessee, west of Creek territory, had also been recognized by the United States. To settle the conflicting claims of the Creeks, Cherokees, and Chickasaws, and to define the actual boundaries of the cession, required negotiation. But instead, Jackson rushed ahead with a survey. The surveyor for this northern and western boundary turned out to be none other than John Coffee, a favorite affinal nephew of Jackson. Coffee had served with Jackson in both the Creek and the Seminole campaigns and was credited with devising the envelopment tactic that was applied to several Creek towns, with devastating results in Creek casualties and property destruction. Coffee's appointment was irregular; furthermore, the survey itself had not been authorized by the other three commissioners, and Coffee had no instructions from the Secretary of War. Nevertheless, Coffee and his surveyors plunged ahead and ran a line defining the entire northern and western boundaries of the cession, over the objections of the Cherokees and the Chickasaws (the Creeks, of course, didn't care). Jackson, as commander of U.S. military forces in the area, even authorized Coffee to raise troops to protect the survey party from angry Indians. Coffee ran the northern line along the Tennessee River (the boundary of an earlier Cherokee cession), thus putting the entire Tennessee Valley south of the river in the hands of the United States. This questionable survey was completed by March 1816.

Jackson and Coffee had tried to conceal these proceedings from the Secretary of War, William Crawford, who was the leader of a Democratic political faction opposed to that of Jackson and his friends. The Secretary discounted the Treaty of Fort Jackson, and therefore the subsequent survey, and moved to resolve the conflicting tribal claims without involving Jackson. In March 1816, he negotiated a treaty with a Cherokee delegation in Washington in which the United States recognized *Cherokee*, not Creek, claims in the Tennessee Valley south of the Tennessee River; the Cherokees in return ceded a small piece of unoccupied Cherokee land in South Carolina. The treaty also allowed the Cherokees payment for damages suffered by them at the hands of Jackson's own Tennessee militia during the Creek War.

The fat was now in the fire. Jackson was enraged; he and the governor of Tennessee protested hotly. But Secretary Crawford responded by ordering Jackson to remove the illegal white squatters on Cherokee land who had been enticed there by Jackson and Coffee. Jackson refused to drive out the squatters and threatened war against the Cherokees. Seizing back the initiative, Jackson arranged a joint treaty with the Cherokees and the Chickasaws (the Creeks and Choctaws refused to attend). At the Chickasaw Council House in September 1816, Jackson as the leading commissioner was able to persuade the attending delegates to *jointly* cede the south-of-the-Tennessee lands to the United States. To accomplish this end, Jackson candidly admitted, it was necessary to bribe the chiefs. A month later, more bribery (and, the Cherokees later charged, forgery) induced the Cherokee national council to ratify the cession.

After the grand expropriation of Creek and Cherokee land in 1814, 1815, and 1816, Jackson served as commissioner at several other treaties of cession. In 1817, he arranged the purchase from the Cherokees of a small tract in Georgia. This treaty was the first to contain an explicit "removal" provision. If a Cherokee contingent should emigrate to new homes west of the Mississippi, to join some three thousand Cherokees already living there, the United States would acquire for the combined group additional land in what is now the state of Arkansas. Actually, Jackson had first demanded that the entire tribe remove to the West. This the delegation refused to agree to, but by dint of bribes and intimidation some six thousand Cherokees—mostly the poorer and least acculturated—were in the next year and a half carried West at the War Department's expense. In 1818 Jackson met with the Chickasaws, and again by threats and bribery certain leading chiefs were persuaded to give up most of the remaining Chickasaw claims in western Tennessee. There was no removal agreement; instead, a few small reservations were allowed, all but one of them actually being private allotments to influential Indians. The national reserve in the ceded tract amounted to only four square miles —so small that the emigration of some Chickasaws would be inevitable. And finally, in 1820, again with threats and bribery, Jackson convinced the Choctaws to exchange part of their remaining land in Mississippi for new territory in Arkansas, and the United States agreed to give them the proceeds from the sale of fifty-four sections of land to establish a school fund for the tribe.

Thus, by the end of 1820, six years after his exploits in the War of 1812 had won him power in national affairs, Jackson had personally forced the Southern Indians to cede much of Georgia, most of Alabama, virtually all of western Tennessee, and a valuable chunk of land in southern Mississippi north of Natchez. These cessions took in about half the territory that had been held by the Southern Indians at the beginning of the war and it opened on the order of 50 million acres to white settlers and speculators.

The Seminoles in Florida, however, had been out of reach of Jackson the land-buyer because Florida was, until 1819, a Spanish possession. That did not stop the impetuous Jackson from personally leading an invasion of Florida in 1818, allegedly to stop the Seminoles from raiding frontier settlements in southern Georgia and providing sanctuary to escaped slaves. After burning some Indian villages and capturing a Spanish fort, he court-martialed and hanged several of the Seminole prophets (probably former Creek Red Stick chiefs). Of the two British subjects, supposedly the instigators of the Indian atrocities, one was hanged and the other shot. Finally, he captured the Spanish town of Pensacola. In reaction to this unauthorized invasion of a Spanish colony, there was talk in Washington of Jackson being publicly censured. But instead, after Spain sold Florida to the United States, Jackson was sent back to Florida as governor!

Before the invasion, in 1817, Jackson had advised his friends and relations that land values in Florida would soon be going up. His business associate James Jackson, the husband of one of Jackson's wards, and his nephew John Donelson purchased thousands of acres of land at Pensacola shortly before U.S. troops crossed the border. Jackson was not happy in Florida, however, and moved back to Nashville, leaving it to his friend and former military associate James Gadsden to negotiate with the Seminoles. The Gadsden Treaty in 1823 procured the cession of most of Florida. John Coffee, of course, surveyed the Seminole reservation, an enormous, landlocked tract in the middle of the territory.

But by 1823, Jackson was caught up in preparations for his unsuccessful bid for the presidency in the campaign of 1824. In 1828 he ran again, this time successfully. And once in Washington, he returned with undiminished determination to the subject of Indian removal.

Andrew Jackson's personal view of the Native Americans evolved over a considerable period of time. As a land speculator, politician, and militia commander from the 1790s through the War of 1812, he had been typical of frontier spokesmen in his rhetorical denunciations of the Indian. The Indians were savage, cruel, bloodthirsty, cannibalistic butchers of innocent white women and children, and should be driven into submission or extinction. But Jackson's relationships with individual Indians could be warm, even intimate. After a battle at the outset of the Creek War in 1814, he adopted a little Indian boy both of whose parents had been killed by his troops. Jackson sent the child, named Lincoyer, home to his wife to be raised in the Jackson household side by side with his adopted nephew,

Andrew Jackson. Jackson referred to Lincoyer as his son and compared the boy's life to his own—both were orphaned at an early age. He apprenticed him to a harness maker, as he himself had been. Unhappily, Lincoyer died of tuberculosis at the age of sixteen. Later, during the war, Jackson set free the Creek military leader Weatherford, who had surrendered voluntarily. And Jackson was not above employing Native American warriors from various tribes in all his military campaigns.

As he came to deal with Indians in the postwar land-cession treaties, Jackson developed a new rhetoric. The Native Americans were now a conquered and dependent people. The object of government must be to save them from imminent extinction by removing them to the West, far from the white settlements, and of course in the process acquiring their lands (some of which, as we have seen, would become his personal property). If possible, their leaders—who he asserted were naturally corrupt and avaricious—should be persuaded by bribes, whether of cash, lifetime annuities, or private reservations (tactfully described as individual allotments) that enabled them to remain behind while the rest of their tribes emigrated. When honest chiefs like John Ross of the Cherokees refused to be bribed, Jackson proposed that the traditional practice of treaty making be discontinued and that Congress should simply legislate the seizure of land not actually occupied by villages. A law disallowing further treaties with Indian tribes and mandating congressional legislation instead was not adopted for another fifty years; but the practice of allotment was extended to Indians in the treaties of the 1830s, on the theory that the holdouts, being improvident by nature, would soon be forced to sell their land and follow their emigrating fellow tribesmen to the West. Referring to the 1817 treaty, which allowed the residents of the ceded lands the option of emigrating either to their fellow tribesmen's lands in Georgia or to their relations west of the Mississippi, or of taking small individual allotments, he observed that "the principle established by the treaty . . . will give us the whole country in less than two years." Only a minute fraction would remain behind permanently, those few who were "pre-pared for agricultural pursuits, civil life, and a government of laws" (i.e., the laws of the state of Georgia). Jackson never proposed exterminating the Indians or, at least in public rhet-oric, removing by force of arms those who wished to remain. But he was adept at devising conditions that would make those who chose not to remove so miserable that they would emigrate eventually anyway. Like many others, he seems to have regarded as inevitable the ultimate extinction of the Native Americans as a culturally distinct entity. Their doom was not to be regretted, however: the present race of Indians had destroyed the once great civilization of the "mound builders," he argued (along with others of the time, including Joseph Smith and the Mor-mons), and now their own decline was only one more episode in the history of the human race.

But whatever were Jackson's private reasons for promoting Indian removal—some combination of political ambition, finan-cial greed, and philosophical rationalization—there remained the political forces that he had mobilized under the banner of the Democratic Party. The exaltation of the common man (meaning, on the frontier, the settler and speculator hungry for Indian land), the sense of America as the redeemer nation destined for continental expansion, the open acceptance of racism as a justification not only for the enslavement of blacks but also for the expulsion of Native Americans—these were popular, politically powerful themes that would have driven any Democratic President to press for a policy of Indian removal.

While Jackson was deploring the continued presence of Native Americans in the Southern states, doomed to extinction there unless saved by removal, the Indians themselves were taking on the trappings, and to a considerable degree the substance, of white culture. It was for them a necessary survival strategy. The losses of the Native Americans in the wars with the whites had been extremely high. Thousands had been killed or wounded in military engagements: for instance, in General Jackson's campaign against the pro-Tecumseh Red Sticks in 1814, about 1,500 Creek fighters were killed. Furthermore, it had been standard white strategy to destroy the Indians' economic and social structure by attacking villages, which were often left virtually undefended, occupied only by women, children, and old men while the warriors were in the field. Soldiers killed indiscriminately, burned houses, destroyed crops, chopped down fruit trees, slaughtered livestock, and drove survivors away to take refuge where they could. Refugee encampments in turn became death traps where starvation and disease cut down hundreds more. By the end of the Indian wars in the spring of 1814, it was clear to the leaders of both the Southern and the Northern tribes that the strategy of resisting white encroachment on Indian land by military means had failed. Continuation of hostilities against more numerous and better-armed opponents could end only in annihilation. A new policy of remaining peacefully on unsold tribal land and adopting white customs seemed, to many of the leading men and women, to be the only road to survival.

Long before 1814, along the coasts and in the interior of New York and Pennsylvania, an acculturative survival strategy had already evolved. Tribes sold land to secure annual payments in cash or manufactured goods like cloth, reserving from the sales sufficient land ("reservations") about the villages to permit agriculture and light hunting. The more "progressive" factions adopted certain white customs, such as male agriculture, keeping livestock, growing new crops, such as cotton in the South and wheat in the North.

In the North, the most visible exemplar of the reservation-and-acculturation policy was provided by the Iroquois of New York. A remarkable cultural transformation had taken place among them soon after the sale of their lands. Partly urged upon them by Quaker missionaries and partly recommended by a Seneca religious prophet named Handsome Lake, a sub-stantial proportion of the men had overcome their aversion to agricultural labor, traditionally regarded as women's work, and had taken to plowing and fencing their fields, raising domestic animals, building separate farmhouses in the white style. Some rafted timber cut in their own sawmill down the Allegheny River to Pittsburgh. A temperance movement, urgently demanded by the prophet, dramatically reduced drunkenness. As early as 1801, using the new agricultural methods, the Indians' yield of corn had increased tenfold. By 1806, new crops were being cultivated, including buckwheat, oats, flax, turnips, and potatoes. By 1813, many of the Iroquois women were spinning linen and woolen yarn and the men were weaving cloth. By 1820, the Seneca settlement at Allegheny, about five hundred souls, was keeping sheep, pigs, chickens, and swine, and hundreds of head of cattle and horses. Henry R. Schoolcraft, who visited the Iroquois in 1845, found an occupational distribution among the men probably not much different from that of nearby white communities: 371 "farmers," 151 "semi-hunters" (i.e., men who supported themselves and their families in part from the chase), 20 "mechanics" (such as blacksmiths, carpenters, masons, wheelwrights, etc.), 35 interpreters, 17 teachers and ministers, 20 men with college or other advanced education, 7 physicians, and 2 lawyers. A decade later, many of the men would become wage workers for the railroads in western New York.

In the Southeast, a similar transformation took place among the five major tribes—the Cherokees, Choctaws, Chickasaws, Creeks, and Seminoles—after 1814. A concerted effort was made by influential chiefs to move toward what both they and white advisors called "civilization." Perhaps their past tradition of administrative centralization, and a high degree of male involvement in agriculture, made it possible for the Southern tribes to change policy without the inspiration of a visionary like the Iroquois prophet Handsome Lake. In any case, the process of culture change among the five tribes was extraordinarily rapid. Missionaries were invited among them to establish English-speaking schools, and substantial funds (for that era) were provided by the U.S. government, at a rate of $10,000 per year, and by the tribes themselves out of annuity payments derived from past land sales, at a rate of about $20,000 per year. Missionary societies, particularly the American Board of Commissioners for Foreign Missions, administered these monies and contributed funds themselves from voluntary donations, primarily by Northern congregations. By 1825, there were eleven such schools among the Choctaws, six among the Cherokees, two among the Chickasaws, and one for the Creeks. A number of the more promising pupils were sent to private academies in the North, where they were trained in the professions as lawyers, physicians, or ministers of the gospel.

Among the Cherokees, the principal school was Brainerd, started in 1817 and supported by the American Board. By 1822, Brainerd was giving board, lodging, and instruction to about one hundred male and female scholars. It had a considerable physical plant: separate schoolhouses for boys and girls, eleven cabins that served as their dormitories, a residence for the white teachers and their families, a dining hall and kitchen, a laundry, a lumberyard, a meat house, a grist mill, a sawmill, and smiths' and carpenters' shops. Select pupils went on to the Board's academy at Cornwall, Connecticut, where Cherokee students rubbed shoulders with scholars from other tribes and from places as far away as Tahiti and India.

Progress in the material arts was also dramatic. An educated and enthusiastic young Christian Cherokee, David Brown, in 1825 wrote to Thomas McKenney, Superintendent of the newly created Bureau of Indian Affairs, describing how prosperous the Cherokee nation had recently become. Their population in Georgia and adjoining states had increased to 15,000 (including several hundred white men with Indian wives). Brown spoke of "numberless herds of cattle," "plenty" of horses, "numerous flocks of sheep, goats, and swine." The Cherokees now were raising corn, wheat, oats, potatoes (both "sweet and Irish"), tobacco, indigo (a plant valuable as a dye for cotton yarn), and cotton. Surplus food was sold to nearby white communities and cotton was exported to New Orleans. There were public roads and inns for travelers. Cotton and woolen cloth was manufactured on local spinning wheels and looms; there were Cherokee mechanics, Cherokee merchants, Cherokee plantation owners who kept slaves to work in the cotton fields. In effect, Cherokee communities, at least in the less mountainous southern part of the Cherokee country, looked very much like white rural communities.

In addition to progress in acquiring white culture, native innovators were contributing to the transformation. In 1821, Sequoyah, a Cherokee silversmith (formerly a professional hunter and fur trader, crippled in a hunting accident), presented to the chiefs a syllabary that he had invented for writing in the Cherokee language. The chiefs supported the idea of rendering the Cherokees literate in their own tongue, and within months thousands of Cherokees, young and old, were able to read and write in syllabary. By 1824, parts of the Bible were being translated and published in Cherokee, and in 1828, a weekly newspaper, *The Cherokee Phoenix*, began to appear, each edition printed in both English and Cherokee.

Similar progress in education and the acceptance of the white man's arts and crafts was reported from the Choctaws, 25,000 of whom lived in Mississippi and Alabama. In 1818, the American Board set up Eliot School in Mississippi, comparable in design and management to Brainerd. The boys at Eliot were instructed according to the Lancastrian plan, the more advanced pupils teaching the beginners; the girls were taught by a missionary. The Reverend Jedidiah Morse, a Congregationalist minister from Boston, in 1820 accepted a presidential commission to make a nationwide survey of the Indian tribes; his *Report to the Secretary of War* was published in 1822. He described the Choctaws as having "strong tendencies toward a civilized state." He reported in a friendly but patronizing way that, like the Cherokees, the Choctaws had made "great advances." They had given up hunting almost entirely and were keeping large numbers of horses and cattle, and were raising all kinds of crops, including cotton. In one year alone they spun and wove 10,000 yards of cotton cloth, using machinery manufactured by a

Choctaw artisan. Again like the Cherokees, they maintained public roads and had established several public inns, which "for neatness and accommodations, actually excel many among the whites."

And Morse had similar praise for the Chickasaws, a much smaller group of about four thousand residents in the northern part of Mississippi, where plow agriculture and animal husbandry also had begun. The Chickasaw chiefs had likewise applied to the American Board for a mission school comparable to that provided for the Cherokees and the Choctaws.

Of the twenty thousand or so Creeks and the more anti-American faction of the Cherokees living in western Georgia, the reports of progress toward civilization were less glowing. "Their minds," explained Morse, were still "irritated by the recent wars" with the United States, and consequently they were less inclined "to receive instruction." But even so, he included them in his rosy, if culturally arrogant, projection. They, too, were raising European crops and keeping livestock and poultry; they, too, had the spinning wheel, the loom, and the blacksmith's anvil; and some of the children were being taught the three R's.

In Morse's opinion, removal and colonization beyond the Mississippi would not be needed for the four most progressive tribes—the Cherokees, the Choctaws, the Chickasaws, and the Creeks. These Southern tribes, he proclaimed, unlike the fragmentary "reduced" tribes to the North, could be "educated where they are, raised to the rank and privileges of citizens, and merged in the mass of the nation." He urged the government to make "the experiment of the practicability of a complete civilization of the Indians."

But as white critics (like Lewis Cass) of this optimistic policy would soon point out, there was a darker side to the story. Most tribes were split into at least two factions, a pro-assimilation "progressive" faction and an anti-assimilation "conservative" faction. They debated fiercely and sometimes came to blows over acceptance or rejection of various white practices, from the Christian religion to English education to metal tools and woven cloth. Missionaries and government agents mostly favored and dealt with the progressive faction, and it was its progress toward "civilization" that observers like Morse reported. But away from the agencies and the schools, and off the main roads lined with cotton plantations and comfortable inns, lived thousands of Native Americans who did not share in this prosperity and who were all too likely to turn to alcohol to dull the pain of poverty and loss. In the South, it would appear, something like an Indian class system existed, perhaps a relic from pre-Columbian times, when differences in rank and privilege were the norm.

But to many whites, especially in Georgia, the threat was not so much the savage, drunken Indian as the civilized one, who if left in place to govern himself in his own territory would beat the white man at his own game—raising cotton—and prevent forever the further acquisition of Indian land.

The economic progress and increasing literacy of the so-called Civilized Tribes was bad enough in the eyes of Southern whites. But worse than all this, in Georgia's eyes, was a change in the form of government adopted by the Cherokees in emulation of federal political institutions. In 1817, the Cherokees had established a bicameral legislature, a chief executive, a judiciary, and a small army. The legislature passed dozens of laws regulating marriage, the tribal treasury, the whiskey trade, legal contracts, and so forth, mostly following white practice. And in 1827, that legislature adopted a new, written constitution (including a bill of rights), modeled after the Constitution of the United States. This constitution asserted that the Cherokee nation was "sovereign and independent."

The economic progress and increasing literacy of the Cherokees were bad enough, but the Cherokee declaration of independence was the last straw for Georgia, and it precipitated a political confrontation between that state and the federal government.

Georgians had long resented the fact that there remained in

the northwestern corner of the state (where John Ross lived) a block of land still in Cherokee hands. Ever since the Revolution, the state of Georgia had sought to establish the principle that Indians did not have a right of occupancy; they were mere tenants at will, who could be removed with or without their consent. Guided by this interpretation, in the 1790s Georgia sold large tracts of land in the future states of Alabama and Mississippi (then administered by Georgia) to the so-called Yazoo land companies. Settlements were planned along the Yazoo River and at Muscle Shoals, along the Tennessee. Grants of land were made to influential public officials, including Andrew Jackson, who in 1797, while a U.S. senator, received 1,000 acres at the Shoals. Jackson had another association with the scheme: his wife's father, Colonel John Donelson, Jr., had been killed by Cherokees resisting an effort by an even earlier land company, headed by territorial governor William Blount, to open a white settlement at the Shoals.

These premature efforts by Georgia and other Southern states to expropriate Indian land were prohibited under both the Articles of Confederation and the Constitution. The United States alone had the authority to treat with the Indian tribes and to acquire their territory, which upon purchase became public lands of the United States, only then to be sold to private individuals and land companies. The Yazoo land titles were thus invalid; speculators stood to lose a lot of money; protests were made to Washington. In 1802, in settlement of the matter, Georgia formally ceded to the United States its western lands (the future Mississippi and Alabama), and the United States in turn agreed to compensate the unfortunate investors in the Yazoo companies, to extinguish Indian title in Georgia, and to turn the lands over to the state to be disposed of as the state saw fit.

But the latter promise was not quickly kept. The Creeks made two relatively small cessions, in 1802 and 1805, of lands in central Georgia. No more lands were acquired until the Creek cession of 1814. Between 1814 and 1826, a series of cessions, largely engineered by Andrew Jackson, cleared the Creeks out of Georgia entirely. But there remained the Cherokees in the northwest corner (north and west of the present city of Atlanta).

Georgia in the late 1820s was a prosperous and rapidly developing commonwealth. The state government encouraged the growth of an extensive system of private banks that lent money to aspiring farmers and entrepreneurs. Family farms were the norm; there were few cotton plantations larger than 500 acres. Railroads and shallow-draft steamboats were opening up the agricultural interior and connecting the cotton country with seaports at Savannah and Brunswick, through which passed the trade not only with Great Britain but also with the industrial Northern states. Georgia was less inclined than her neighbor South Carolina to espouse the doctrine of nullification, so hateful to President Jackson, propounded by that state's legislature and advocated by her native son Vice President John C. Calhoun. Increasingly, too, the Georgia electorate was turning away from the faction headed by Jackson's old political rival, William H. Crawford, and was favoring the party more friendly to the President. Jackson had motives for rewarding Georgia that went beyond his commitment to Indian removal.

Thus Georgians felt that they had the right to claim the President's sympathetic attention in time of need. And now was that time. The Cherokee constitution in effect nullified Georgia law and made the Indian nation a "state within a state." Left to themselves, the Cherokees would become a prosperous, independent commonwealth, and they would never sell their land (indeed, by Cherokee law, the further sale of land to the United States was a crime). On December 20, 1828, immediately after the election of Andrew Jackson as President of the United States, the Georgia legislature passed a law extending the state's jurisdiction—i.e., its laws, its police powers, and its courts—over the Cherokees living within the state. Enforcement was to be deferred until June 1, 1830, to give the President and Congress time to act in support of Georgia.

*   *   *

Georgia's action forced the President's hand. He must see to it that a removal policy long covertly pursued by the White House would now be enacted into law by the Congress. The new President quickly took steps to implement a removal program that would, among other things, resolve the Georgia crisis. As his Secretary of War he appointed his old friend and political supporter from Tennessee, Senator John Eaton. No doubt with the advice of Superintendent McKenney, who had convinced himself of the need for removal, Eaton included in his first (1829) Report to the President a recommendation for wholesale removal of the Eastern Indians to a self-governing "Indian territory" in the West, where the U.S. Army would protect them from intruding whites and keep the peace among the tribes.

The Twenty-first Congress convened for its first session in December 1829, and as was (and still is) the custom, the President delivered to it a message reporting on the State of the Union and making recommendations for new legislation. Not unexpectedly, he paid considerable attention to the Indian question (see Appendix A). About half the discussion of Indian affairs was devoted to the constitutional issue raised by the Cherokee claim to independence and political sovereignty within the state of Georgia. Jackson stated that in his view the Native Americans residing within the boundaries of old or new states were subject to the laws of those states. He recognized the efforts of some tribes to become "civilized" but saw the only hope for their survival to be removal to a Western territory. The rhetoric was candid but compassionate in tone, no doubt intended to disarm criticism, suggesting that removal was not merely legally justified but morally necessary, and that he was responding not to the greed of land speculators and would-be settlers but to a moral imperative to save the Indians from extinction. Emigration, of course, should be strictly voluntary with individuals. Those who chose to leave would be provided with an "ample district West of the Mississippi," to be guaranteed to them as long as they occupied it. Each tribe would have its own territory and its own government and would be free to receive "benevolent" instructors in the "arts of civilization." In the future, there might arise "an interesting commonwealth, destined to perpetuate the race, and to attest the humanity and justice of this Government." For those who chose to remain, he gave assurance that they would "without doubt" be allowed to keep possession of their houses and gardens. But he warned them that they must obey the laws of the states in which they lived, and must be prepared to give up all claims to "tracts of country on which they have neither dwelt nor made improvements, merely because they have seen them from the mountain, or passed them in the chace." Eventually, those who stayed behind could expect to "become merged in the mass of our population."

On February 24, 1830, a removal bill was reported out from the House Committee on Indian Affairs (John Bell of Tennessee, chairman). The same bill was also introduced into the Senate by its Indian Committee (also chaired by a Jackson man from Tennessee). The text of the bill (see Appendix B) was briefer than the President's message recommending it. In eight sections, it authorized the President to set aside an Indian territory on public lands west of the Mississippi; to exchange districts there for land now occupied by Indians in the East; to grant the tribes absolute ownership of their new homes "forever"; to treat with tribes for the rearrangement of boundaries in order to effect the removal; to ensure that property left behind by emigrating Indians be properly appraised and fair compensation be paid; to give the emigrants "aid and assistance" on their journey and for the first year after their arrival in their new country; to protect the emigrants from hostile Indians in the West and from any other intruders; to continue the "superintendence" now exercised over the Indians by the Trade and Intercourse Laws. And to carry out these responsibilities, the Congress appropriated the sum (soon to prove woefully inadequate) of $500,000.

The debate on the bill was long and bitter, for the subject of Indian removal touched upon a number of very emotional issues: the constitutional question of states' rights versus federal prerogatives, Christian charity, national honor, racial and cultural prejudices, manifest destiny, and of course just plain greed. The opening salvo was the Report of the Indian Committee of the House. The report defended the constitutional right of the states to exercise sovereignty over residents, including Indians, within their borders. It discussed the nature of Indian title, naïvely asserting that in pre-Columbian times "the whole country was a common hunting ground"; they claimed as private or tribal property only their "moveable wigwams" and in some parts of the continent "their small corn patches." The committee declared that the Indians were incapable of "civilization," despite their recent "extravagant pretensions," so loudly touted by misguided zealots opposed to emigration. Among the Cherokees, the report asserted, only a small oligarchy of twenty-five or thirty families controlled the government, and only these, and about two hundred mixed-blood families who made up what the report referred to as a "middle class," could claim to have made any progress toward what the committee regarded as "civilization." These favored few opposed emigration. But the remainder, allegedly living in indolence, poverty, and vice, were generally in favor of removal as the only way to escape destitution and eventual annihilation. Obviously, in the committee's view, it was not merely justifiable but morally imperative to save the Southern tribes from extinction by helping them to emigrate to the West.

Both Houses of Congress were deluged by hundreds of petitions and memorials, solicited by religious groups and benevolent societies opposed to Indian removal. Town meetings were held, particularly in the Northern states, demanding justice for the Native Americans. Joseph Hemphill, congressman from Pennsylvania, published a review of Cass's article "Indian Reform," excoriating him for recommending an oppressive policy toward the Indians; and he included in his condemnation the Reverend Isaac McCoy, who had written a book, *The Practicability of Indian Reform*, urging removal as the only means of civilizing the natives. The American Board of Commissioners exerted wide influence on Protestant denominations in the cause of Indian rights. Not to be outdone, friends of Jackson organized their own pro-removal missionary society, its masthead adorned with the names of prominent officials and clergymen who favored the bill. Its efforts were eclipsed by the older American Board, however, whose leader, Jeremiah Evarts, under the *nom de plume* William Penn, had already published his *Essays on the Present Crisis in the Condition of the American Indians*.

In the spring of 1830, active debate began in the chambers of Congress. The attack on the bill was launched in the Senate by Theodore Frelinghuysen of New Jersey, a distinguished lawyer whose deep religious convictions had already earned him the respect of colleagues in both parties. Frelinghuysen, a Whig, was an example of the "Christian party in politics," for at one time or another he was president of the American Board of Commissioners for Foreign Missions (sixteen years), president of the American Bible Society (sixteen years), president of the American Tract Society (six years), vice president of the American Sunday School Union (fifty years), and for many years an officer of the American Temperance Union and the American Colonization Society. His stand on the Indian question was to earn him a national reputation as "the Christian statesman" and in 1844 a place on the Whig ticket as (unsuccessful) candidate for Vice President of the United States, along with Henry Clay for President. Senator Frelinghuysen's speech, which took three days to deliver, pointed out that the Indian policy of the United States, from the time of Washington on, had been based on the principle that the United States was obligated to protect peaceful natives living in unceded territory from intrusion by whites under any pretext, by force if necessary. Treaties with the Native Americans, according to the Constitution, were, like other treaties, the law of the land. The Jackson Administration, by refusing to enforce existing treaties, was violating the Constitution.

Why was more Indian land needed now, when annual sales of public lands amounted to no more than 1 million acres? The

Indian occupants of the continent had already peacefully sold more than 214 million acres, and much of that remained vacant. To be sure, hunters would eventually sell to agriculturists, but willingly and in response to reasonable argument, not by coercion, as this bill, in the hands of this administration, promised. Furthermore, many of the Native Americans, in response to the official reform policy of the United States government, were adopting white customs and could be expected to amalgamate with the whites, if left alone where they were. Frelinghuysen concluded with an essentially moral appeal:

> Sir, if we abandon these aboriginal proprietors of our soil, these early allies and adopted children of our forefathers, how shall we justify it to our country? . . . How shall we justify this trespass to ourselves? . . . Let us beware how, by oppressive encroachments upon the sacred privileges of our Indian neighbors, we minister to the agonies of future remorse.

The pro-removal reply to Frelinghuysen was delivered by Senator John Forsyth of Georgia. Like his opponent, Forsyth was a lawyer and a former attorney general of his state. He had served as a representative in Congress, as minister to Spain (he secured the King's ratification of the 1819 treaty ceding Florida to the United States), and, most recently, he had served as governor of Georgia (1827–29). He was a loyal Jackson follower, would later support Jackson and oppose Calhoun over nullification, and in 1834 he was rewarded by appointment as Secretary of State. He was a skilled orator and had the reputation of being the best debater of his time.

Forsyth dismissed Frelinghuysen's words as a mere self-interested plea by the "Christian party in politics" to create unwarranted sympathy for the Indians, among whom their missionaries lived so prosperously. He pointed to the deplorable conditions under which the Native Americans now lived and to the long history of the removal policy. Forsyth, as a true friend of the Indians, had long had doubts that removal would promote their civilization, but he would vote for this bill because it would relieve the states "from a population useless and bothersome" and would place these wild hunters in a country better supplied with game. But most of Forsyth's time was spent on legal arguments about states' rights (particularly Georgia's) to exercise sovereignty over Indians, about old treaties and proclamations, and about natural law. He concluded that Georgia had a right to expect the United States to remove the Indians (without coercion, of course) to a happier hunting ground west of the Mississippi.

The debate raged for weeks in both the Senate and the House. Amendments were proposed in the Senate that would have weakened the bill by protecting the Indians' interests; three times these amendments were defeated by a single vote. In general, delegates from the Northern and Eastern states, many of them National Republicans, anti-Masons, and moral reformers, stood against the bill, and Southern and Western delegates—many, like Jackson, with little interest in evangelical Christianity—favored it. Eventually, on April 23, 1830, the Senate voted 28 to 19 to pass the measure. On May 24, the House passed the bill by a narrower margin, 102 to 97.

President Jackson signed the Removal Act on the same day. It was, some maintained, the "leading measure" of his administration; indeed, "the greatest question that ever came before Congress, short of the question of peace and war." Jackson himself said that Indian removal was the "most arduous part of my duty" as President.

A fairly clear federal policy with regard to the transfer to white owners of title to newly purchased Indian lands, based on a generation of experience, was already in place when the Removal Act was passed and signed. In some cessions, individual Indians were allowed to retain small tracts, called "allotments" (in distinction to tribally owned "reservations"), generally small parcels of land around their residences. These allotments could be sold by their Indian owners to settlers or land companies by government-approved contract. The remainder of the ceded territory became part of the public lands of the United States (except for Georgia, where, by special agreement, lands purchased by the United States were turned over to the state). The usual practice of the federal government was to dispose of the public lands as quickly as possible. The lands were first surveyed and then sold, a large proportion initially at public auction at a minimum price of $1.25 an acre, and the remainder at subsequent privately arranged sales.

Meanwhile, "actual settlers" would be entering these public lands, staking out claims, building cabins, making improvements. Along with the squatters, "land lookers" sent by land companies were prowling about, identifying the best locations for speculative investment. The government did not try to stop the squatters, who often were tacitly accorded a "preemption right" to 80 or 160 acres around their improvements at the minimum price of $1.25 an acre. "Speculator" land companies, while they were condemned in political rhetoric as unfair monopolistic competitors of the "actual settler," at least sometimes supported the settlers' interests. Government did not really want to discourage the speculators any more than the settlers. After all, many politicians and officials (as we have seen, including Jackson and his friends) were speculators in Indian lands themselves, and anyway, there were rarely enough settlers on hand to buy up all the land offered for sale. Besides, some tracts like town sites required expensive development before resale to "actual settlers."

The government did not expect to realize much if any profit from the sale of the public lands. Some of the less desirable tracts, slow to move, eventually went for as little as 12½ cents an acre after languishing for up to five years. Some of the more attractive sites, on the other hand, might bring prices at auction well above the $1.25-an-acre minimum. But even though the Indians would be given only a few cents an acre for their land, the government was likely to agree to pay for the expense of their relocation out of the proceeds from the sale of their former domain. And there were costs associated with preparing the public lands for sale: surveys, the opening of roads, and the operations of the Land Office itself, both in Washington and in the field. Public policy was to get the public lands into private hands, for economic development, as quickly as possible.

Thus the Jackson administration was ready to do its "land-office business" as soon as the Indians could be persuaded to sell and agree to remove. In fact, efforts to that end were already under way.

4

THE TRAIL OF TEARS

RESPONSIBILITY for arranging the actual removal of the Indians was now in the hands of the administration. Jackson had in place a removal team: his protégé John Eaton, the Secretary of War; Thomas McKenney, Superintendent of the Indian Office, a declared supporter of removal; General Coffee, his old comrade-in-arms, always ready to serve as the situation demanded—as Indian fighter, treaty negotiator, or surveyor of purchased lands. He also had available the staff of Indian agents who served under McKenney. But McKenney, despite his support for the principle of voluntary removal, soon balked at the harassment tactics of the administration. He was removed from office in August 1830. In 1831, after another official had served for a year, the position was filled by a loyal Jacksonite, Elbert Herring, who supported the removal policy until he left in 1836. Along with McKenney, about half the experienced Indian agents in the field were replaced by Jackson men. They could be counted on to execute administration policy more readily than those whose long acquaintance with Native Americans had made them too sympathetic. In 1831, Eaton, mired in an embarrassing domestic scandal, was replaced as Secretary of War by Lewis Cass, who, as we have seen, was not only a loyal Democrat but also a leading advocate of removal. Not incidentally, his political leadership in the Michigan Territory, which was about to become a state, would come in handy at election time in 1832.

It was the team of Jackson, Cass, and Herring that supervised the removal of most of the Southern Indians from 1830 through 1836. By the end of 1836, the Choctaws and Creeks had emigrated, and by the close of 1837 the Chickasaws had followed. Cherokee resistance was not broken, however, until 1839, and the Seminoles were not removed until 1842, after a long and bloody war.

In principle, emigration was to be voluntary; the Removal Act did not require Native Americans to emigrate, and those who wished to remain could do so. But the actual policy of the administration was to encourage removal by all possible means, fair or foul.

Jackson as usual spoke publicly in a tone of friendship and concern for Indian welfare. In a letter of instruction to an agent who was to visit the Choctaws in October 1829 (even before the Removal Act was passed) he outlined the message from "their father," the President, urging them to emigrate. The threats were veiled. "They and my white children are too near each other to live in harmony and peace." The state of Mississippi had the right to extend a burdensome jurisdiction over them, and "the general government will be obliged to sustain the States in the exercise of their right." He, as President, could be their friend only if they removed beyond the Mississippi, where they should have a "land of their own, which they shall possess as long as Grass grows or water runs . . . and I never speak with forked tongue."

A harsh policy was nevertheless quickly put in place. To weaken the power of the chiefs, many of whom opposed removal, the traditional practice of paying annuities in a lump sum, to be used by the chiefs on behalf of the tribe for capital improvements and education, was terminated and annuities were doled out piecemeal to individual Indians. The amounts were pitifully small—each Cherokee was to receive forty-four cents per year, for example, and even that was to be withheld until he reached the West. Some annuities were not paid at all, being diverted by local agents to pay spurious damage claims allowed by state courts against Indians.

The principal acts of harassment, however, were carried out by the governments and citizens of the Southern states. The extension of state sovereignty over the tribes within their borders led quickly to the passage of destructive legislation. The tribal governments, so carefully organized in imitation of white institutions, were simply abolished; it became illegal for tribes to establish their own laws and to convict and punish lawbreakers. The chiefs were to have no power. Tribal assemblies were banned. Indians were subject to state taxes, militia duty, and suits for debt. Indians were denied the right to vote, to bring suit, even to testify in court (as heathens all—despite the evidence of conversion for many—they could not swear a Christian oath). Intruders were encouraged to settle on Indian territory; lands were sold even before they had been ceded. In Georgia, after gold was discovered on Cherokee property, the Indians were prohibited from digging or mining gold on their own land, while hundreds of white prospectors were allowed to trespass and steal the gold with impunity.

And all the while, the federal government stood idly by, refusing to intervene in the application of state laws. The result was chaos. Thousands of intruders swarmed over the Indian country in a frenzied quest for land and gold, destroying Indian farms and crops. The missionaries tried to persuade their Indian friends to stand firm against removal. But Georgia passed a law requiring missionaries to take an oath of loyalty to the state or leave the Indian country, and when a number refused, they were seized, imprisoned, tried, convicted, and sentenced to long prison terms. All but two were pardoned after they signed a pledge to obey the laws of Georgia. The recalcitrant ones, the famous Samuel Worcester, former head of the American Board's school at Brainerd, publisher of *The Cherokee Phoenix*, and an ardent anti-removal advocate, and an assistant missionary, Elizur Butler, chose to appeal their convictions. While they languished in prison, the case wound its way up to the Supreme Court, where the issue was interpreted in the context of Georgia's claim of state sovereignty. The Supreme Court found against Georgia's right to supersede federal authority over Indian tribes and thus set aside Georgia's assertion of state sovereignty over the Cherokees and their missionaries. Jackson was not impressed, however, and is reputed to have said, "Justice Marshall has made his decision, now let him enforce it." Whether he actually used these words has been questioned; but they represent his sentiments, for the administration did nothing to aid the missionaries or effectively to deter intruders. Worcester was not released from prison until the following year (1833).

The other major legal challenge to the state's sovereignty was an earlier suit pressed by the Cherokee nation that directly challenged the constitutionality of Georgia's attempt to execute state law within the Indian country. Former Attorney General William Wirt (who also represented Samuel Worcester) applied to the Supreme Court for an injunction. But this case was dismissed on the technical ground that an Indian nation was not a foreign state but a "domestic dependent nation," a "ward" of its "guardian," the United States, and therefore could not bring suit before the Supreme Court.

It is abundantly clear that Jackson and his administration were determined to permit the extension of state sovereignty because it would result in the harassment of Indians, powerless to resist, by speculators and intruders hungry for Indian land. Jackson, of course, was not always so indulgent of states' rights, as is shown by his famous threat later on to use military force against South Carolina if that state acted on John Calhoun's doctrine of nullification.

Shortly after the passage of the Removal Act, Congress adjourned for the summer. The President and his Secretary of War, John Eaton, left Washington for a vacation at their homes in Tennessee, to be joined there later by General Coffee. Jackson, however, intended it to be a working holiday. He was determined to initiate the removal process by personally negotiating emigration agreements with the Southern tribes, and accordingly messages were sent to the Choctaws and Chickasaws in Mississippi, the Creeks in Alabama, and the Cherokees in Georgia, inviting them to meet with their Great Father at Franklin, Tennessee, where Eaton lived; Jackson's estate, The Hermitage, was nearby.

The invitation was rejected outright by the Creeks and Cherokees; as we have seen, they hoped to block the government's colonization plan by appealing to the Supreme Court. The Choctaws also chose to stay away. A delegation of Chickasaws did arrive late in August, and to them Jackson was able to deliver his address. He urged them to exchange their lands in Mississippi for a new home in the West. He warned that he could not shield them from the harsh laws of the state in which they now resided, and further warned that if they delayed in accepting his offer to pay the expenses of removal and to support them for the first year in their new settlements, future emigration would have to be done without help from the government. He understood their deep attachment to the land of their fathers, but alas, if they remained, they would soon cease to exist as a nation, they would disappear and be forgotten. It was up to them to decide, in consultation with Eaton and Coffee, who would furnish them with more detailed information.

The Chickasaw chiefs, bribed by Eaton and Coffee with offers of private reservations in Mississippi, decided to accept, and a treaty was signed on August 31, 1830. But the Senate refused to ratify the treaty and Chickasaw removal was delayed until a new treaty could be signed, an event that did not occur until 1832.

Eaton and Coffee were now dispatched as emissaries to the Choctaws, to meet them in their own country and try to negotiate a treaty there. The Choctaws were deeply divided, not only over removal, but also over the extent to which they should adopt white culture. Chief Greenwood LeFlore, one of the so-called

mixed-bloods who pressed for acculturation and even amalgamation with the whites, and who was the patron of the most
effective missionary schools, favored signing a removal treaty,
but many of the common people and some of the other chiefs
opposed it. Eaton and Coffee removed some of their objections
by the liberal use of bribes, paying out money and providing
over fifty influential men with private reservations in Mississippi.
LeFlore and the other two principal chiefs each received a four-
square-mile tract. Medals and gifts were handed out, and
eventually the Indians still present—for many had returned to
their homes in disgust—agreed to sign.

The Treaty of Dancing Rabbit Creek between the United
States and the Choctaws was signed on September 27, 1830. It
was the first of the land-exchange treaties under the Removal
Act to be ratified by the Senate and its provisions put into effect.
In return for ceding all their land east of the Mississippi (less
the private reserves), amounting to about 11 million acres, the
Choctaws were to receive a tract of land bounded on the east
by the Arkansas state line, on the south and west by the border
between the United States and Mexico (later Texas), and on the
north by the Canadian fork of the Red River, encompassing
over 15 million acres stretching across the southern half of the
present state of Oklahoma. Reconnaissance parties reported
that it was a fine country, well watered, with fertile soil, plenty
of cane (needed for building houses), and stands of excellent
timber.

But the Choctaws had a disastrous experience in the actual
emigration. The first misfortune was a result of the machinations
of Greenwood LeFlore. Even before the treaty was ratified,
LeFlore was actively persuading the owners of private reservations to sell, and common people to vacate their homes, and
was encouraging white settlers to take possession immediately.
The displaced families belonged to LeFlore's Christian faction,
which included many of the more acculturated and affluent
Choctaws. They started out for the West in the fall of 1830,
shortly after the treaty was signed, without escort by government

agents or troops, and with minimal logistical preparation. They were accompanied by two missionaries. In all, LeFlore sent out about a thousand people; during the winter, only eighty-eight reached the intended settlement on the Kiamichi River, near an abandoned military post (Fort Towson) on the Red River, in the extreme southeastern corner of the Choctaw tract. These survivors, who were mostly women and children, had struggled for months through unfamiliar country during the coldest winter on record, assisted only by their two missionaries, who spent hundreds of dollars of their own money to buy food and other necessaries from white settlers in Arkansas. (The government later refused to reimburse the missionaries for these expenditures because they had not been authorized in advance.) They arrived in their new homes near starvation. Although the military commander at Fort Gibson, on the Arkansas River north of the Choctaw tract, sent down a detachment to help the Indians by rebuilding the old fort and buying food for them, this help did not arrive until spring. Later, in the summer, about four hundred of the winter stragglers arrived.

The conservative, anti-missionary faction among the Choctaws was led by an old chief named Mushulatubbe, one of LeFlore's political rivals. Mushulatubbe was an old friend of Andrew Jackson's, having served under him in the Creek War and later at the Battle of New Orleans. He had two wives, one at each of his two plantations, and he owned eleven slaves and large herds of cattle and horses. Mushulatubbe and his people did not want to settle near the Christian villages on the Kiamichi River, and so when he and his followers arrived in the West, they established themselves near Fort Smith on the Arkansas River, in the northeastern corner of the Choctaw tract.

Emigration of these more conservative Choctaws continued throughout 1831 and 1832. About four thousand made the trek in that period, traveling in parties of several hundred to a thousand or more, some of them escorted by troops and agents with money to pay emergency expenses. Private companies arranged transportation and provided rations. Parties would start out on steamboats, which carried them up the Mississippi and in some cases the Arkansas River, but all finally had to reach their ultimate destination by overland marches of two to four hundred miles. Those who had to trek overland during the winter suffered the worst. The winter of 1831–32 was as bad as the one before and the sufferings of the emigrants were severe. Those who chose to travel without government assistance, in order to qualify for a $10 per capita remuneration at the end of their journey (or because they were afraid to travel in dilapidated old steamboats, with their notorious propensity for explosions and fires), probably suffered the most.

One party of three hundred who elected to emigrate on their own crossed the Mississippi at Vicksburg and headed north along the road beside the river, sixty-eight miles to Lake Providence, where they were to find a cache of provisions. Along the way they had to endure what a local resident called "the worst time of weather I have ever seen in any country," and the bad weather continued, with rain, sleet, and extreme cold. The party then proceeded westward toward the next cache of provisions, eighty miles, fifty of which lay through a great swamp with no road. About forty miles into the swamp they became lost and could proceed no longer. When they were at last found by an emigration agent, they had had no food for six days, and most if not all of their 1,500 horses and 50 yoke of oxen had died; hundreds of horses and many of the oxen were seen "standing up in the mud stiff and dead." And this incredible journey was being taken by old women, old men, and children, most of them without so much as moccasins on their feet, wearing light cotton summer clothing, supplied with only one blanket per family. The agents managed to rescue 265 people and 227 horses and cattle. They were escorted to the nearest town, given shelter in a rented schoolhouse, and finally put on board a steamboat that took them two hundred miles up the Ouachita River to an assembly point at Ecor à Fabri. Thence they marched overland to the settlement area along the Red River near Fort Towson.

Not all the Choctaw emigrating parties experienced such extreme suffering. Some were carried most of the way by steamboat. Those who traveled with special agents and military escort were better supplied and guided. And to avoid the rigors of winter travel, a large number chose to emigrate during the summer. But summer had its own dangers. Those who emigrated during the summers of 1832 and 1833 were engulfed by the cholera epidemic that swept across the United States in those years, and thousands died. If the mortality throughout the Choctaw population stood at the level of 20 percent reported for the group settled along the Arkansas, then on the order of four thousand Choctaws must have died of cholera, in addition to the hundreds who perished from hunger, exposure, and accidents along the way.

The emigration of the Choctaws ground to a halt after the summer of 1833. About nine thousand had reached Indian territory; about seven thousand remained in Mississippi, most fleeing into the woods and swamps. The prosperous few were accepted in white society. A few thousand more were persuaded to emigrate in the 1840s, but other thousands stayed where they were.

The War Department was the government agency responsible for assisting the various tribes in their removal to the West. The disastrous experience (in both human and financial terms) of the first efforts at the Choctaw removal, resulting in large part from a confusion of military and civilian areas of responsibility, prompted Secretary of War Cass to formulate tighter and clearer rules that placed future removals entirely under the supervision of the military. In the spring of 1832, new regulations were issued that specified the respective roles of the military command on the one hand, and private contractors on the other. The army's Commissary General of Subsistence—in 1832, General George Gibson—was to be in charge of all removals. Senior officers were to be appointed as special agents to supervise the removal of each tribe. They would report weekly to the War Department. These agents would make all decisions with regard to the route and mode of transportation. By land, the émigrés would proceed on foot, with wagons, one for every fifty persons, to carry the young, the infirm, and the baggage (an average of thirty pounds per person was the maximum allowed). If the special agent chose to send the emigrants by water, he was authorized to rent the paddle-wheel steamboats now common on Western rivers. Supplies were to be provided by private contractors approved by the commissary general and were to be placed in caches along the route. Agents were instructed to issue about a pound of beef, pork, or salt pork per person per day, plus corn, flour, and salt. And the special agents were authorized to employ junior officers to escort each emigrating party in person. These officers would pay for all emergency supplies (such as food or clothing) and services (such as medical care and extra transportation) required along the way, and were to submit financial records and a journal to the War Department at the end of each trek. Indian houses, farms, farm equipment, and other property left behind would be sold at well-advertised public auctions and the proceeds remitted to the tribes for distribution to the former owners.

These revised regulations ameliorated the conditions under which at least one of the subsequent removals of Southern Indians was carried out: that of the Chickasaws.

It was not until October 1832 that General Coffee was able to persuade the Chickasaws to sign a treaty selling all their land east of the Mississippi—the northeastern corner of the state of Mississippi and a small sliver of Alabama. They were expected to use the proceeds to buy land from the Choctaws; although the Choctaws were reluctant, they eventually (in February 1837) agreed to assign the western part of their country to the Chickasaws, at a price of $530,000, and to accept them as citizens of their nation. Coffee also required the Chickasaw tribe to assign small reservations of land in Mississippi to each family; the Indians protested, but to no avail. Immediately after the treaty was signed, speculators, squatters, and whiskey sellers crowded into the Chickasaw country, even before the official

survey had been completed, and bought up the Indian allotments for a few dollars apiece. The Chickasaws remained in
Mississippi, suffering with this situation, for five years, from
1832 to 1837, while they waited for the agreement with the
Choctaws to be signed.

The actual emigration of the Chickasaws was not as disastrous
as had been the case with the Choctaws. Both Indians and the
government had learned from that terrible experience and the
new regulations were in place. Better land transportation was
available, roads had been built, supplies cached along the way,
more adequate quantities of blankets, shoes, and clothing provided. By the end of 1838, about six thousand Chickasaws had
located along the tributaries of the Red River, west of the
Choctaws; only a few hundred remained in Mississippi, and
most of them departed in the next few years.

Although the Creeks had refused to treat with Jackson in 1830
on the subject of removal, intruders flooded into the Creek
country, confident that Alabama courts would never convict
them and that the federal government would not intervene.
Whiskey sellers plied their trade with impunity and alcoholic
Indians sold off their few worldly goods to obtain liquor. Land
speculators and squatters marked Indian agricultural lands for
future settlement when the inevitable cession of land would
legalize their trespass. At last the Creek chiefs, realizing that in
spite of all its past promises the federal government would not
protect them, sent a delegation to Washington that, on March
24, 1832, ceded to the United States all the Creek lands east of
the Mississippi River in exchange for a new home in the West,
where they expected to live in peace and govern themselves.

There were certain provisions in this treaty, however, that
would lead to disaster. Each Creek Indian was free to emigrate
or not, as he or she saw fit. Furthermore, each head of family
was to be allotted 320 acres that would include his own house
and fields, and the ninety chiefs were each entitled to 640 acres
or one square mile. The Creek nation in 1833, according to a

census taken in that year, had a population of 22,690 (including 902 black slaves), with 6,557 heads of families. The sum of the allotments thus amounted to 2,187,200 acres, nearly half the 5,200,000 acres owned by the tribe in Alabama. The owners of these reserves were free to sell and emigrate; if at the end of five years some still wished to remain in Alabama, they would be given a deed to the property. Sales of the reserves were subject to the approval of the President. All intruders were to be kept off Indian land for five years; but to encourage Creeks to enroll, the government agreed to pay the costs of emigration, to support the emigrants for a year in the West, and to give each man a rifle and ammunition, and each family a single blanket. And to make it easier to leave Alabama, the government agreed to pay up to $100,000 to settle the private debts of Creek Indians.

The provision for individual, salable reserves, and the promise to pay the Native Americans' debts to whites, promptly unleashed a new torrent of intruders onto the Creek lands. Many Indians had indeed gone into debt to buy whiskey and merchandise; unscrupulous traders added fraudulent claims; threats to sue could not be resisted because Indian testimony would not be admitted in a state court. Mobs of squatters ran the Indians out of their villages, burned their houses, seized their crops and livestock, and left the families destitute and starving in the woods. By the summer of 1833, there were estimated to be three thousand illegal intruders in the Creek country; the next year, the number had grown to ten thousand.

The federal government did make some effort to evict the intruders, but the effort was ineffectual. Secretary of War Cass would order the military to drive the intruders off; a few would be ejected, but they would return almost immediately; and the white population grew more and more hostile. A crisis erupted over the eviction of one Hardiman Owen, who had physically beaten Indians, driven them from their lands, shot their cattle and hogs. Owen attempted to murder the marshal executing the eviction order by blowing him up with gunpowder; the attempt failed (the marshal was warned by an Indian) and Owen was shot and killed by a soldier when he resisted arrest. A county grand jury then indicted not only the soldier but also the marshal, other soldiers, and the commanding officer at Fort Mitchell on charges of murder. Armed conflict between U.S. troops and Alabama militia seemed likely. To defuse the situation, Jackson dispatched Francis Scott Key to mediate the dispute, and eventually a compromise was reached, the federal government agreeing not to enforce its promise to keep intruders off Creek lands and the state agreeing to try to prevent speculators and others from harassing the Indians and to drop charges against the marshal and the troops from Fort Mitchell.

Worse was still to come: the infamous land frauds. The land frauds concerned the 320-acre reserves allotted to the 6,557 heads of families. When an Indian wished to sell, he and the buyer were to appear before an agent appointed to witness the transaction. The Indian would identify himself and describe his holding (through an interpreter, in most cases) and the buyer would hand over payment. Then the agent would write down the details and send the document to Washington for the President's approval. A number of these "certifying agents" were appointed in November 1833 and they began their work in January 1834.

A scheme of massive fraud commenced almost at once, devised by companies of land speculators from Columbus, Georgia (just across the state line). The speculator would hire a stray Indian to testify that he was the owner of a particular reserve (whose real owner was not then interested in selling). He would pay the Indian a pittance, frequently a mere ten dollars, for 320 acres of prime farmland (the minimum price for public lands at this time was $1.25 an acre). The agent, who might or might not know any better, would certify the conveyance to the President. The same Indian might be used again and again; and the same reserve might be fraudulently purchased over and over by different buyers. The speculator would then sell the property to a settler, who would proceed to drive the innocent and unsuspecting true Indian owner and his family off their land. It is estimated that half of all the reserve conveyances were obtained by this kind of fraud.

The outcry against these proceedings came not only from the Creeks, who protested in writing to the President, but also from local white observers, whose vivid descriptions of the frauds perpetrated on the Creeks were published in local newspapers. Reports reached Washington from the field agents and the military; newspapers across the country spread word of the scandal. At last the President was persuaded to act. He appointed a commissioner, John B. Hogan, an Alabama resident and a trusted friend of the Indians, to investigate. Hogan's account was scathing: "A greater mass of corruption, perhaps, has never been congregated in any part of the world, than has been engendered by the Creek treaty in the grant of reservations of land to those people." In March, Secretary of War Cass appointed Hogan and two other commissioners to make an even more serious investigation, in order to rectify the frauds and to clear up the morass of faulty land titles that threatened to plunge Alabama real estate into endless litigation.

But the investigation was never to be completed. The situation of the Creeks, driven from their lands and homes, sick and starving in the woods and swamps, was desperate. Already there had been many incidents of violence, both by and upon the Indians. On May 16, 1836, a more serious turn of events took place: a band of fifty or sixty men, allegedly Indians, waylaid a stage carrying U.S. mail on the road between Columbus, Georgia, and Tuskegee, Alabama. This, following upon a number of murders and depredations by Creeks in the neighborhood of Columbus and Tuskegee, produced something akin to panic. The opinion of responsible community leaders, as expressed editorially by the *Montgomery Advertiser*, was that the Indian outbreak had been directly instigated by the speculators in order to block Hogan's investigation; and in fact, a white man was later tried, convicted, and sentenced to hang for having incited the Indians to attack the stage. But nevertheless, when news of the attack reached Washington, Secretary Cass instructed Hogan's commission to abandon the fraud investigation and he ordered General Thomas S. Jesup to mount a military campaign against the hostile faction, subdue them, and then remove the entire tribe, by force if necessary, to their new country west of the Mississippi.

The Second Creek War, as it was called, did not take long. By July, the hostile Indians had been captured, the eight hundred warriors manacled and chained, and they and the remainder—women, children, and old men—were being marched under military guard to Montgomery, Alabama, where they were put on boats for transportation West. Upward of 3,000 "hostiles" set out; hundreds died along the way of disease and accidents, and about 2,300 finally arrived at Fort Gibson. These survivors, observed a compassionate army officer, were in a state of "total destitution . . . [I have] never seen so wretched and poor a body of Indians." They were provided with axes and other hardware, and placed, not without protest, under the governance of Chief McIntosh, who had emigrated with his faction in 1829. So ended the Second Creek War.

The rest of the Creek nation followed shortly after, with some notable exceptions. The peaceful Creeks, who had taken no part in the hostilities, asked for the payment of their annuities in advance to defray the cost of the emigration and to help in setting themselves up in a new land. General Jesup refused to allow this unless the Creeks sent a detachment of six hundred to one thousand warriors to help the U.S. Army fight the Seminoles in Florida. The survivors of this force eventually rejoined their brethren in the West. Nearly all the remainder of the tribe were transported West during the fall and winter of 1836–37 and the summer and fall of 1837.

The removal of the peaceful Creeks was a wretched affair from beginning to end. Although they traveled under military escort—which served more to protect the Indians than to harass them—the responsibility for provisioning them and securing the wagons and steamboats for travel was given to a private company, the Alabama Emigrating Company, which received a fixed amount for the job and was therefore motivated to do as little for their charges as possible. The Indians traveling in winter were forced to endure snow, sleet, and freezing cold without adequate shelter or clothes in their way across Arkansas. By the end of 1837, about eighteen thousand "friendly" Creeks had joined the "hostiles" and the McIntosh Creeks in the West.

There was one last sad event that further illustrates the needless tragedy of the Creek removal. The Emigrating Company hired a decrepit old steamboat, the *Monmouth*, to transport 611 Indians up the Mississippi from New Orleans. The captain steered his boat into a one-way channel reserved for descending vessels. There she collided with another steamship and was cut in two; 311 of the Indians on board were killed.

Estimates of the total loss of life in the process of Creek removal from 1832 to 1838 have ranged as high as ten thousand. While this seems to be an excessive percentage (45 percent of the tribe), undoubtedly thousands perished as victims of starvation, disease, exposure, accidents, murder, and wounds received in military combat.

In 1830, most of the Cherokees still remained in the East, to the number of sixteen thousand or more. There was, however, already a sizable contingent of "Western Cherokees" living in Texas and Arkansas. Some had emigrated as early as 1794 and became the nucleus of the Texas band; another group settled along the Arkansas River in 1816, and in 1828 they and the government signed a treaty providing for their removal from what would become the state of Arkansas and their resettlement farther west in Indian territory. The Western Cherokees were joined in 1830, even before the Removal Act, by about five hundred more émigrés, so that the number of Cherokees living across the Mississippi in that year was on the order of four thousand.

The Cherokees still in the East, however, were not about to be moved. Led by their principal chief, John Ross, they undertook, as we have seen, to challenge the legality of the oppressive laws of Georgia and to appeal to Andrew Jackson, Lewis Cass, and their local Indian agents to enforce what they understood to be the protective guarantees embodied in previous treaties, which, according to the U.S. Constitution, were the law of the land. But the administration flatly refused to act, informing the Indians that they would have to obey Georgia law.

Fully aware that the President did not intend to intervene on behalf of the Indians, Georgia proceeded on its path of nullification of federal law and its harassment of the Cherokees. Cherokee lands were declared to be state property, they were surveyed, and in 1832 they were officially sold in the state lottery. Hundreds of white families occupied farm sites in anticipation of their title being legalized by the state. Some of the plantations of the wealthier Indians were simply expropriated.

Meanwhile, the federal establishment maintained pressure on the Cherokees to remove to the West, even without a removal treaty. Jackson ordered agents to enroll individual Cherokees for transport to the West under the provisions of the 1828 treaty. The chiefs countered that move by threatening dire punishment for any who did enroll, and rejected the government's proposal of a removal treaty. When Jackson personally suggested paying the tribe $3 million for all their lands except those in North Carolina, Chief John Ross turned him down. By the summer of 1834, no more than a thousand Cherokees had left for the West, despite the repeated efforts of federal agents to encourage wholesale emigration.

The continued pressure to move and the relentless harassment by the state were having one effect, however: to create factionalism. Although the majority of the chiefs' council, led by John Ross, remained adamantly opposed to leaving their homes, a sizable opposition to their policy was beginning to develop, led by Chief Major Ridge, his son John Ridge, and Elias Boudinot, the editor of *The Cherokee Phoenix*. Ross and Ridge had much in common. Both spoke English fluently and were highly successful plantation owners in the manner of Southern gentlemen, with comfortable houses, fields, slaves, and assorted investments in profitable ventures. Both were pro-Christian progressives. Both had served under Jackson's command in 1814, leading Cherokee troops against the Creeks. Both had risen to positions of influence in the Cherokee nation, Ross as principal chief and Ridge as speaker of the council. Ross's wife was pure Cherokee. Ridge's wife was Cherokee, too, and a confirmed Christian as well.

At first the two men had agreed in opposing emigration. But as the situation worsened in the Cherokee country, Ridge came to the conclusion that the only chance for the survival and continued progress of the Cherokee nation was removal. His was a minority view within the council and within the general population, but he probably had many silent supporters who were afraid to speak out or to enroll for removal out of fear of retaliation from John Ross's majority party.

The existence of even a small pro-removal faction gave the administration the opportunity it needed. In June 1834, a combined delegation of Eastern and Western Cherokees came to Washington to ask the government to set up a line of military posts in Indian territory to protect the Western Cherokees, and such of their Eastern countrymen as chose to join them, from attack by the "wild Indians" of the Plains. They also wanted money to support a peace mission among these Western tribes. John Eaton, Jackson's friend and former Secretary of War, was appointed to treat with them, and he managed to get them to sign a removal treaty, even though the delegates were not authorized to negotiate land exchange and removal. The Senate never ratified the treaty, however, and it was repudiated by the Cherokee council at a meeting called by John Ross. The life of one of the delegates was threatened and a removal advocate in the council was shot to death.

In February 1835, two delegations, the one against removal led by John Ross and the other for removal led by Major Ridge's son John, made their appearance in Washington. The Reverend John F. Schermerhorn, as U.S. Commissioner, met with the younger Ridge and his delegates and got them to sign a treaty by which the Cherokees sold all their lands east of the Mississippi for the sum of $4,500,000 (the Ross party had demanded $20 million). The agreement was to take effect as soon as the Cherokee council approved it. Schermerhorn spent the summer and fall of 1835 in the Cherokee country, trying without success to persuade the chiefs to agree to the treaty. He proposed to Secretary of War Cass to bribe the chiefs, but Cass, to his credit, turned down this suggestion. The council met in October and formally rejected the Schermerhorn treaty.

Georgia and the federal government turned up the pressure another notch. John Ross, about to leave for Washington to work out a more favorable treaty, was arrested by Georgia militia and kept in jail for twelve days without being charged. Arrested along with Ross was the popular journalist John Howard Payne, author of "Home, Sweet Home!," who happened to be a guest in Ross's home at the time, gathering material for a book about the Cherokee country. The office and presses of *The Cherokee Phoenix* were also seized by the guard. And the whole nation was summoned to appear at the former national capital, the town of New Echota in Georgia, in December to approve a new treaty. In anticipation that anti-removal sentiment would induce many to boycott the meeting, circulars announced that all those who did not attend would be considered as voting in favor of removal.

When the Reverend Mr. Schermerhorn got to New Echota in December, he found only three to five hundred men, women, and children; none of the principal chiefs who opposed removal were there. With this rump parliament, headed by pro-removal chiefs Major Ridge and Elias Boudinot, he purported to nego- tiate a treaty, which, despite furious protests from John Ross and other chiefs, the U.S. Senate ratified by one vote. This infamous Treaty of New Echota provided that the Cherokees would abandon all their lands east of the Mississippi and remove to the West within two years. In exchange, they would be entitled to occupy the 7 million acres in Indian territory, north of the Creek line, that had been allotted to the Cherokees in an 1833 agreement with the Western band, plus an additional 800,000 acres.

There was an immediate outcry from Native Americans and from such noteworthy public figures as John Howard Payne, Ralph Waldo Emerson, and Sam Houston of Texas (himself an adopted Cherokee). General Ellis Wool, the officer appointed to oversee the Cherokee removal, repeatedly pointed out to his superiors the fraudulent character of the treaty, the lawless plundering of the Cherokee domain by white intruders, and the Indians' steadfast determination to die rather than leave their country. But he was personally rebuked by the President for harboring views "so disrespectful to the Executive, the Senate, and the American people." President Jackson was determined to press the issue. He advised the Cherokees that he no longer considered them to have a national government, and in order to stifle opposition he prohibited further council meetings to discuss the treaty and ordered federal troops into the region to prevent opposition. General Wool promptly ordered all Cherokees to surrender their guns.

There was a flurry of compliance with the removal treaty. Some three hundred of the people who had gone to New Echota and approved the treaty left promptly for the West, no doubt in fear of their lives. In January 1837, a party of about five hundred, including some of the wealthiest families, left on a land trek to their new homes in the West, and in the fall of 1837, another small group of nearly four hundred departed, traveling by land through Tennessee and briefly stopping along the way to visit Andrew Jackson, now retired from the presidency and living at The Hermitage.

More and more intruders were pushing their way into the Cherokee country, now that the deadline was approaching. General Wool tried to protect the Indians, according to what he understood to be the government's promise, but his efforts to drive out the white invaders prompted the governor of Alabama to charge him with crimes under state law. A military court of inquiry, ordered by the new President, Martin Van Buren, exonerated him. The governor of Georgia threatened armed conflict with the U.S. troops if the Indians were not promptly removed. And still John Ross held fast, demanding an investigation of the fraudulent treaty; Van Buren refused the request. And when in February 1838 Ross presented a petition to the Senate purportedly signed by 15,665 Cherokees (i.e., by every man, woman, child, and infant in the nation), the Senate tabled it.

The deadline for voluntary removal was May 23, 1838. On that date, only about 250 Indians were assembled at the agency, prepared for removal; the rest of the Cherokee population, about 17,000 souls, remained in their homes. The military was prepared to use force, and it did. General Winfield Scott, who had replaced Wool, was put in command of seven thousand regulars and militiamen and ordered to round up the dissidents. And so began the Cherokee "trail of tears," one of the worst episodes in the history of United States relations with Native Americans.

The process was swift and brutal. Detachments of soldiers arrived at every Cherokee house, often without any warning, and drove the inhabitants out at bayonet point, with only the clothes on their backs. Later, they were assured, they would receive a fair compensation for their household goods, farm equipment, and houses. The captives were marched to hastily improvised stockades—in language of the twentieth century, concentration camps—and were kept there under guard until arrangements could be made for their transportation by rail and water to the Indian territory west of the Mississippi. By the end of June, about five thousand had been shipped out, still under guard.

The summer of 1838 was very hot and dry. Drought interfered with securing provisions for the emigrants, and so General Scott agreed to postpone further movement until the fall. Conditions in the stockades were poor and the imprisoned Indians suffered from malnutrition and contracted dysentery and other infectious diseases. The horror of the situation appalled the regular army officers charged with executing the removal plan. In the fall of 1838, General Scott accepted a sensible proposal by Ross that the remainder of the Cherokees be permitted to arrange and supervise their own trek, by land. Scott stood by his word on this agreement despite protests by the President and the Secretary of War. In all, thirteen or fourteen separate parties made the trip by land, each accompanied by a physician and a small military escort. Private contractors were hired to provide food for a total of about thirteen thousand people, five thousand horses, and numerous oxen. Cherokee warriors served as police to maintain order on the march and to prevent whiskey sellers from entering the camp grounds. Six hundred and forty-five wagons were purchased to transport goods and supplies and to carry the very young, the old, and the sick. The first party left Georgia in October 1838; the last arrived at Fort Gibson in March 1839. Although the trip was arduous, especially for a population wearing light summer clothing, the experience was no worse than what the Choctaws, Chickasaws, and Creeks had undergone previously.

But the total cost in Cherokee lives was very great. Perhaps as many as a thousand of the emigrants died en route (including John Ross's wife), and it is estimated that about three thousand had died earlier during the roundup and in the stockades. In all, between 20 percent and 25 percent of the Eastern Cherokees died on the "trail of tears."

Among all the tribes that the government wanted to remove, the most violent resistance was put up by the five thousand Seminole Indians of Florida. They had long been a thorn in the flesh of the white citizens of Georgia, Alabama, and Mississippi because for generations they had accepted and protected, in a condition of mild servitude, hundreds of slaves who had escaped from harsh masters and fled south to live with the Native Americans. Furthermore, the Seminoles themselves were refugees, not the aboriginal inhabitants of the peninsula. They were Creeks who over the years had left their tribe to seek asylum farther south; many had separated from the rest of the nation after the defeat by Andrew Jackson in the War of 1812. A chronic border warfare had long festered in northern Florida, fueled by white insistence on recovering escaped slaves, and as we have seen, Jackson had actually invaded Florida in 1818 just before Spain ceded the province to the United States.

There had been one major land cession by the Seminoles before the Removal Act was passed in 1830. At the treaty of Fort Moultrie, negotiated by Jackson's friend and comrade in arms Colonel James Gadsden in September 1823, certain Seminole chiefs had agreed to sell all the tribe's land in Florida, except for reservations in the northern panhandle, where the chiefs themselves lived, particularly along the Apalachicola River. In turn they accepted a very large, land-locked reserve in central Florida extending from Lake Okeechobee northward to the neighborhood of present-day Ocala. Only the northern edge of this tract was cultivable by native methods of agriculture, and accordingly its boundary was twice extended to the north and east by executive order (as provided in the treaty) to provide additional arable land. The second extension was surveyed in 1826 by the ubiquitous Major Coffee. Few Seminoles moved into the large reserve, however, and then only into the northern part; many remained in their old towns in the panhandle, in spite of constant friction with whites.

In 1832, Colonel Gadsden negotiated a second treaty with the Seminoles. He was a familiar figure to them, having represented the government at the earlier treaty and having surveyed the reservation and recommended its enlargement. The Treaty of Payne's Landing (a site just north of the big reserve) was a removal treaty. Circumstances made it difficult for the Seminoles to refuse: many were in a starving condition, the result of drought, and Colonel Gadsden informed them that only by joining the Creeks in the West would they be permitted to receive their annuities in the future. Under duress, the Seminoles agreed to sell all their remaining land in Florida and to join the Creek nation west of the Mississippi, provided that a delegation to be sent to examine the Western territory reported back favorably, and that the Seminole chiefs in council in Florida then endorsed the report. But when the chiefs in the reconnoitering party reached Fort Gibson, they were shown a copy of the Treaty of Payne's Landing so altered as to read that the exploring party itself had the authority to confirm the treaty. The leaders were persuaded by, among others, the Reverend John Schermerhorn to sign a document committing the tribe to removal within three years, even though they had serious misgivings about the location, which they considered to be too near the "wild Indians" of the Plains. One of them, John Blunt, who had served as Andrew Jackson's guide during the First Seminole War and who had been rewarded with a reservation for himself and his band along the Apalachicola River in 1823, was bribed with the sum of $3,000 and a promise of another $10,000 when he and his band emigrated. And another party to the transaction, the federal agent for the Seminoles, was later dismissed by the government for embezzling tribal funds.

The Seminole chiefs in Florida protested loudly but in vain. The government insisted that the treaty now be enforced and that all the Seminoles emigrate within three years. This confrontation led directly to the Second Seminole War, a war which a large part of the general public, and many of the military officers involved, believed had been caused directly by the fraudulent Treaty of Payne's Landing.

By the time the three-year limit ran out, only a few Seminoles had actually left Florida, principally from John Blunt's Apalachicola band, 152 of whom departed in 1834, not for Indian territory, but for Spanish Texas. The remainder of the five thousand Seminoles sat tight in their thirty or so little villages in the northern part of the large reserve, mostly clustering about the agency near the northern boundary. When time ran out, in the fall of 1835, they still had made no effort to cooperate with removal agents; the deadline was extended to January 8, 1836, but this gesture met with no response except the assassination of a chief who had spoken in favor of removal. Troops were mobilized at Tampa Bay to round up the recalcitrants and remove them by force if necessary.

The first shots of the Second Seminole War were fired on the grounds of the Seminole Agency on December 28, 1835, and it was the Seminoles who drew first blood. Forty or fifty Mikasuki warriors led by a young Creek named Osceola assembled at Fort King, the site of the agency, and shot to death agent Wiley Thompson, a Lieutenant Smyth, and three other men. Osceola had a personal score to settle: he blamed agent Thompson for the kidnapping and enslavement of his wife, and in addition sought to avenge himself for having been put in chains by Thompson when he spoke out against removal at a peaceful parley. Farther south on the same day, a large band of Indians and blacks ambushed Major Dade and his company, who were proceeding north by road from Tampa Bay to reinforce the troops at Fort King and to aid them in the removal of the Indians when the deadline passed. Of the 110 officers and men in Major Dade's command, only three survived. A few days later, another pitched battle took place in which U.S. troops killed thirty to forty Indians.

The issue was now joined. About five hundred "friendly" Seminoles defected from the nation and took refuge at Tampa Bay, whence they were eventually transported by water to the West. The "hostiles" were determined to fight it out. Militias were called out from Florida and other Southern states; they were joined by detachments of regular troops; and a desultory campaign ensued that resulted in some casualties on both sides but had no effect at all on the Seminoles' determination to remain in Florida. The Northern villages, being vulnerable to attack from nearby military posts and readily accessible by existing roads, were abandoned, and the Indians retreated southward into swamps and forests where they were difficult to discover and even more difficult to attack. From these remote strongholds, small war parties issued forth to burn farms, kill white families, and destroy small, isolated military detachments.

The army, for its part, holed up in its string of forts, sallying forth now and then in futile pursuit of the enemy. A truce was negotiated and broken by both sides, and it became apparent that the war was becoming a stalemate.

In Washington, it was now realized that it would require a major military effort by the United States to defeat the Seminoles. In the spring of 1836, a senior military officer, Major General Winfield Scott, was placed in command. Scott had had some experience in Indian warfare: he had fought in the War of 1812 and in the Black Hawk War in 1832, but he was no more successful than his predecessors, and after a few months he was relieved of his command and sent north to chastise the Creeks in the Second Creek War, and after that he was put in charge of the military removal of the Cherokees. He went on to achieve national prominence a decade later in the war with Mexico, and in 1852 ran unsuccessfully as the Whig candidate for President.

General Thomas Jesup replaced Scott and remained in charge of the Florida campaign until the summer of 1838. The thousands of officers and men under his command were no more successful, militarily, than they had been before, under Scott, and the frustrated general turned to less conventional methods to effect removal. Jesup repeatedly invited segments of the Seminole population to meet with him, and when they arrived, under a flag of truce, he found one pretext or another to seize them and forcibly transport them under guard to Tampa Bay, whence they were carried off by steamboat to New Orleans and the West. The blacks were separated from the Indians and checked over by slave traders looking for fugitives, and many were thus recaptured, while others were left to rejoin their Creek friends. The army was able to kill only a few dozen warriors, however, and to capture in the course of military operations only about four hundred men, women, and children. All in all, Jesup reported the removal of nearly two thousand Indians by the end of 1838. This left perhaps two thousand hostile Seminoles still defying the United States; but they were

in increasingly desperate circumstances. Jesup had waged a war
of attrition, and in his final report he stated:

> The villages of the Indians have all been destroyed; and
> their cattle, horses, and other stock, with nearly all their
> other property, taken or destroyed. The swamps and ham-
> mocks have been every where penetrated, and the whole
> country traversed from the Georgia line to the southern
> extremity of Florida; and the small bands who remain
> dispersed over that extensive region, have nothing of value
> left but their rifles.

The war, however, was becoming increasingly unpopular with
the American people, as reports of mounting casualties, widespread outbreaks of infectious diseases, and arduous conditions
in the field made the removal of a few thousand Indians seem
less and less important. The image of thousands of young
soldiers, far from home, wading through swamps in water up
to their necks for days at a time, chasing an ever-retreating
"enemy" who simply wanted to be left alone, did not please the
public. Furthermore, the justice and even the common sense of
the war were widely questioned, and not among the religious
groups alone who had originally criticized the Removal Act.
Even General Jesup, in a letter published in the *Army and Navy
Chronicle*, denounced the war as unnecessary, unjust, and im-
possible to win.

> In regard to the Seminoles, we have committed the error
> of attempting to remove them when their lands were not
> required for agricultural purposes; when they were not in
> the way of the white inhabitants; and when the greater part
> of their country was an unexplored wilderness, of the
> interior of which we were as ignorant as of the interior of
> China . . . My decided opinion is, that unless *immediate*

emigration be abandoned, the war will continue for years to come, and at constantly accumulating expense.

He even officially recommended to the Secretary of War that the war be ended and the Indians allowed to remain in a reservation that included the Everglades and the southern part of Florida.

Despite his opposition to the war he was ordered to wage, Jesup is perhaps best remembered for having made a martyr, and something of a public hero in the Northern press, of the Seminole leader Osceola. Osceola, although not a traditional chief, was the inspirational spokesman for the hostiles. When he attended a council with Jesup under a flag of truce, the general had him seized, put in irons, and shipped off to Charleston, South Carolina, where he remained in confinement until the end of his life. His portrait was painted by George Catlin, along with other Seminoles imprisoned at Fort Moultrie. And proud Osceola's death—of malaria and a throat complaint—was described in detail for a public eager to shower compassion upon victims of governmental oppression.

The commander who replaced Jesup was Colonel Zachary Taylor. A rigorous officer cast in Jackson's mold, Taylor systematically went about solving the logistical problems that had plagued his predecessors, dividing the combat theater into twenty-mile squares, building roads and forts, and establishing an effective occupation of much of the Seminole country. After a year he was replaced by General Alexander Macomb. An indication of the political importance of ending the Seminole War is the fact that Macomb was commanding general of the United States Army. Taylor and Macomb were able to remove another thousand or so Seminoles, but the war dragged on, despite efforts to effect a truce, until 1842, when the United States unilaterally declared it to be over and gave the surviving Seminoles permission to stay, supposedly temporarily, in Florida.

The peace—to which the Seminoles had not formally agreed—ended six years of carnage for both sides. About five hundred Seminoles remained in out-of-the-way villages in the swamps of the Everglades, where their descendants remain to this day. About four thousand had been relocated to the Indian territory, on an allotment north of the Creek tract. Perhaps a thousand or fifteen hundred had died during the course of the war, of wounds, accidents, and disease. For the government, the Florida campaign had been a costly lesson in tropical warfare, comparable (considering the much smaller size of the American population in the 1830s) to the Vietnam War more than a century later. As many as 30,000 troops had been committed, and about 1,500 of these had died, in combat or of disease, and thousands more suffered the permanent effects of wounds and chronic diseases, particularly malaria. Twenty million dollars (an enormous sum at that time) had been spent to remove five thousand Native Americans from a wilderness where whites had no wish to settle anyway. But for some officers, the war was a stepping-stone to success. General Winfield Scott, as we have said, went on to achieve fame as the conqueror of Mexico City, and later was a candidate for President on the Whig ticket. Colonel Zachary Taylor also became prominent during the Mexican war, succeeded Macomb as commanding general of the U.S. Army, and in 1848, after his decisive victory at Buena Vista during the war with Mexico, was elected twelfth President of the United States. And young Lieutenant George Gordon Meade, just graduated from West Point, was detailed in 1836 to escort a group of Seminoles to Fort Gibson. Perhaps disillusioned with this duty, he resigned his commission later that year and entered upon a career as civil engineer. Later he rejoined the service and in 1863, as the newly appointed commander of the Army of the Potomac, defeated the Confederates at the Battle of Gettysburg. During Reconstruction, he returned to the South, heading the military administration of Georgia, Alabama, and Florida.

THE LONG SHADOW
OF THE REMOVAL POLICY

THE Five Civilized Tribes had a very difficult time in their first years in the West. Old factional disputes over "civilization," over religion, and over tribal policy toward federal and state governments had hardened into armed confrontation and led to some bloodshed. Among the Cherokees, for example, the chiefs who had signed the Schermerhorn treaty, in defiance of a Cherokee ban on further sales of land under penalty of death, were marked for revenge. After their arrival in the Indian territory, Major Ridge, his son John Ridge, and Elias Boudinot were lynched by anti-removal vigilantes. Most of the tribes' capital goods—metal tools and equipment, firearms, traps, horses and oxen—had been left in the East or lost en route, and partly in consequence of this, the immigrants chose to settle at first in the near vicinity of the military posts, particularly Fort Gibson and Fort Coffee on the Arkansas River and Fort Towson near the Red River, where they could acquire new farming equipment, food, clothing, and other necessaries. The forts would also serve to protect them from the feared "wild Indians"—Plains tribes, like the Comanches and the Pawnees, who lived in large part from hunting and raiding—and from the intrusion of unwanted white men like whiskey sellers. Matters were not helped by a succession of bad winters, floods, and droughts in the thirties and forties.

Nevertheless, the "progressive" factions among the Five Tribes persevered in working to reestablish the kinds of communities that they had built in the East. The settlements year by year moved farther inland, up the principal rivers. Missionaries were invited to return and establish schools. Capital goods were purchased with annuities and solicited from the government. Inter- and intratribal disputes and grievances were gradually settled. The Cherokees were perhaps the most successful in restoring themselves to some degree of prosperity and order. By the mid-1840s, plantations and farms had been reestablished; the former republican constitution was in force, and the seat of government organized at Tahlequah, near Fort Gibson on the Arkansas River; hundreds of pupils were attending both public and religious schools; the Reverends Butler and Worcester, whose arrest and jailing by the state of Georgia had caused a national furor a decade before, were at work again—Dr. Butler running a boarding school for both boys and girls and Dr. Worcester operating the publishing house that the Georgia authorities had suppressed, producing both religious and secular books, and issuing the national weekly newspaper, *The Cherokee Advocate*, in both English and Sequoyah characters.

But not all tribesmen participated in these advances. Among the Cherokees, perhaps six thousand constituted a prosperous, literate middle class; but there were thousands who still lived in rural poverty, and the proportion of those in destitute circumstances among the other tribes was considerably higher. The majority of the population of the Five Civilized Tribes probably never regained the level of comfort that they had enjoyed back East. They were living in a harsher environment, subject to greater extremes of temperature, flood, and drought. Instead of the traditional town complexes with surrounding fields, there were now scattered farms, and the traditional, lightly constructed winter and summer houses had been replaced by the "two-pen" house, an arrangement of two one-room log cabins connected by an open, roofed passageway.

Another difficulty was dissatisfaction with the enforced consolidation of different tribes on common territories. The Choctaws and Chickasaws chafed under the arrangement, and in

1855 the two tribes officially separated and agreed on a mutual boundary. The assignment of the Seminoles to Creek lands and governance also was unsuccessful from the start, and a treaty of partial separation was signed in 1845 and one providing for complete partition in 1856.

The persistence of tribal separatism also ran counter to proposals made by self-declared friends of the Indians that the Indian territory be made into an official territory of the United States, destined, like the other territories, to graduate into statehood. Such a territory would, of course, have to be ruled by a single territorial administration under supervision of the federal government and thus would require a subordination of tribal sovereignties to some sort of intertribal council. Suggestions for the creation of an Indian "state in embryo" had been seriously put forward during Monroe's and Adams's presidencies. Well-known authorities on the Native Americans, including Jedidiah Morse, Isaac McCoy, and John Schermerhorn, pleaded forcefully for territorial organization, and after removal, bills were repeatedly introduced in Congress to establish territory status for the Indians in what eventually became the state of Oklahoma. These proposals all failed of passage, however, partly because they were regularly opposed by the Indians themselves, and partly because many whites hoped that Indian territory would eventually be opened to white economic exploitation. After the Civil War, the government tried to impose a union on the Five Civilized Tribes, but they were only able to enforce a compromise, a weak "general council." In the 1870s, President Grant suggested putting all the Indians in the country into "one Territory or one State," but the plan was not carried out.

One outcome of these grand schemes for an all-Indian territory was to diminish the lands in possession of the Five Civilized Tribes. As a punishment for siding with the confederacy, the five tribes were required, in treaties held in 1866, to give up the western portion of their domain, in order to provide a new home for various displaced Western Indians. The tribes were not averse to giving asylum to various remnant groups from the East, and had incorporated elements of such disparate bands as the Shawnee, Delaware, and Seneca from the Northeast, and the Natchez and Catawba from the Southeast. And in 1855, as part of the Choctaw-Chickasaw settlement, these tribes conveyed to the United States a territory in the western part of their domain, to be known as the "leased district," for the resettlement of tribes from Texas. But now they were confronted with an influx of strangers from the West. Eventually, the Indian territory bulged with the arrival of Pawnees, Kiowas, Comanches, Wichitas, Cheyennes, and others from the Plains, as well as Osages and more from Kansas and Nebraska and Texas. Captives taken by the U.S. Army in wars in the Far West were brought to the territory, too: Modocs from California in 1873, Nez Perces from Oregon and Idaho in 1878, and Chiricahua Apaches from Arizona in 1889. The Indian territory, after the Civil War effectively restricted to what would become the state of Oklahoma, had become a place of exile for Indians from all over the United States whom the government considered to be inconveniently located. Elements of no fewer than sixty tribes, in addition to the Five Civilized Tribes, eventually were moved into Oklahoma.

The Northern tribes suffered less from the removal policy, and that suffering was postponed longer than was the case with the Southern Indians. Some communities were never moved at all. President Jackson was less interested personally and there was less political pressure from the Northern states. Many of these "nations" numbered merely a few hundred souls occupying much smaller reservations than those in the South. Others, more numerous, lived in the remote forests and lakes of northern Michigan, Wisconsin, and Minnesota. Actual removal did not begin for most until after Jackson left the presidency, and even then it was usually only partly carried out.

Nevertheless, as it had in the South, the federal government moved promptly to extinguish Indian title to land in the Northeastern states. In a series of treaties from 1831 to 1836, the Shawnees, Senecas, and Ottawas in northern Ohio ceded their tracts and prepared to join their brethren in the West. The Miamis agreed in 1840 to leave Indiana. In northern Indiana, Illinois, and southeastern Wisconsin, in treaties from 1832 to 1834, the Ottawas, Potawatomis, and Chippewas agreed to grant millions of acres in exchange for lands across the Mississippi. The Wyandots held out the longest, clinging to their 110,000-acre reserve on the upper Sandusky River near Lake Erie until 1842, when they, too, sold and agreed to remove. In southern Wisconsin, the Menominees and Winnebagos also signed removal treaties in the 1830s and '40s.

But the pace of actual removal of the Northern tribes was much slower than had been the case in the South. By 1842, when the Second Seminole War ended and the last major group of captives left for Indian territory, the Miamis still clung to their reservation in Indiana; the Ottawas and Chippewas remained virtually undisturbed around the northern lakes in Michigan, Wisconsin, and Minnesota; Winnebago fugitives still evaded removal in southern Wisconsin; and the Senecas refused to leave their disputed reservations in New York State.

The principal source of resistance in Indiana came from the Miamis, a broken-down and demoralized fragment of a once-great confederacy, who obstinately clung to their "Big Reserve" on the south side of the Wabash. In 1840, their chiefs had been persuaded to cede their 500,000 acres in Indiana in exchange for an equivalent tract in Indian territory, and they were given five years to remove. They stalled, however, and in 1846 were escorted to the West by the U.S. Army. But about half the tribe evaded the troops, and many of those who were transported to the West surreptitiously returned to Indiana. As late as 1950, about seven hundred Miamis still remained in Indiana.

The Menominees and Winnebagos in Wisconsin also proved to be difficult to dislodge. The Menominees did not sell all their tracts in Wisconsin until 1847, when they agreed to remove northward onto lands made available by the Chippewas. But they refused to vacate, and eventually a reservation was provided them within the state, where their descendants still reside, along with some Oneidas, Mahicans, and Munsees to whom the Menominees had given shelter well before 1830.

The Winnebagos also were difficult to remove. Although they had agreed to move west of the Mississippi at the treaty of 1832, many still had not left by 1837. In that year a conference was held in Washington, supposedly about other matters, with Winnebago delegates who were not authorized to sell land. These unfortunate men were detained until the approach of winter, when their concern about the welfare of their families persuaded them to sign away the tribe's remaining lands east of the Mississippi and to agree to remove to the West. They were deceived by the government interpreter, who told them that the tribe would have eight years to complete the removal, while the text of the treaty—enforced by the United States—read "eight months." To add to the Winnebagos' discomfort, a presidential commission was appointed to look into debt claims by fur traders, particularly the American Fur Company. Of the $300,000 disbursed by the commission, it was charged that between $60,000 and $100,000 was pocketed by the commission's chairman, the notorious Pennsylvania politician Simon Cameron. Half the tribe refused to go and led a fugitive life in Wisconsin, periodically being rounded up by troops and shipped off to wherever their brethren happened to be in the West, only to slip back into Wisconsin again. Their situation was eventually legalized in the latter part of the century, when they were able to secure private titles to tracts scattered over ten counties in central Wisconsin, under the Homestead Act when it was extended to Indians in 1875.

Part of the federal animus against the Winnebagos may have derived from their support of the Sac leader Black Hawk and his band, who, inspired by the nativistic preachings of a Winnebago prophet, in 1832 reentered former Sac territory at Rock Island, Illinois, and terrorized local white settlers. Pursued by Illinois militia, whom they routed in an initial engagement, and eventually by units of the U.S. Army, they attempted to escape to the North and to recross the Mississippi. The band, including men, women, and children, was slaughtered at the crossing by fire from steamboats, and the survivors who reached the western bank were hunted down by Sioux warriors. The leader, Black Hawk, lived to tell the tale in a widely read autobiography and became something of a national hero (like Osceola) with his defiant declaration "I am a man!"

Although the northern parts of Michigan, Wisconsin, and Minnesota were less attractive for settlement, the government proceeded to attempt to clear these areas of Indian title, too. In 1836 Lewis Cass's protégé, Henry R. Schoolcraft, agent to the Chippewas in northern Michigan, who later became a popular writer on Indian subjects, negotiated a treaty with the Ottawas and Chippewas that extinguished Indian title to most of northern and western Michigan. A number of reservations were left, scattered through the territory, and although the Indians agreed to send a deputation to look for suitable sites for resettlement west of the Mississippi, they were officially allowed to remain relatively undisturbed for many years. Other major cessions were made by the Chippewas of their remaining lands in northern Michigan and northern Wisconsin in the 1840s, with the usual provision for scattered reservations at summer village sites. But the Chippewas could always retreat north and west into the as yet untouched wilderness of Minnesota, where 90 percent of the land was still owned and occupied by Sioux and Chippewas as late as 1850.

The other major holdout was the Seneca nation, which owned and occupied four substantial reservations in western New York. These reserves had been created at the federally supervised Treaty of Big Tree in 1797, when the Senecas sold the bulk of their remaining lands between the Genesee River and Lake Erie to the Holland Land Company. The Holland Land Company retained an option to buy these reserves when the Senecas were willing to sell, and the successor to the Holland Company, the Ogden Land Company, acquired the option. By 1838, Ogden was becoming anxious to buy the Senecas' increasingly valuable real estate.

The effort to remove the peaceful and inoffensive Senecas became a *cause célèbre* that symbolized, in the opinion of many Northern white people, the fraudulent and cruel nature of the Indian removal policy. It also produced a revolution in Seneca society itself. The Seneca case is worth examining in some detail because it galvanized public sympathy for Native Americans caught in the trap of removal and because it led directly to a more careful and sympathetic study of Indian cultures by observers like Lewis Henry Morgan, the father of modern American ethnography.

The Reverend John Schermerhorn was appointed treaty commissioner for the purpose of arranging the cession. But the Senecas were almost unanimously opposed to the sale of their lands. As we have seen, many had made substantial progress toward what whites would call "civilization," they were at peace with their neighbors, and were so small a population—on the order of 2,500 souls, living on four reservations amounting altogether to about 200 square miles—as to constitute very little threat to the continued development of the Empire State.

In 1838, Schermerhorn and representatives of the Ogden Land Company decided to force a treaty upon the unwilling nation. They collected a few chiefs and a number of other men at an inn on one of the reservations, Buffalo Creek (where the city of Buffalo now stands), plied them with whiskey and bribes, and persuaded these debauched individuals to sign a treaty selling all the Seneca lands and the reservation of their guests, the Tuscaroras, to the Ogden Land Company, for the sum of $202,000. They also agreed that the whole nation would remove west into Indian territory in what is now the state of Kansas within five years. Although the fraud was quickly denounced by both Indians and well-disposed whites, and even President Van Buren initially refused to accept the treaty, returning it to the Senate with a message outlining its improper nature, the

Treaty of Buffalo Creek was finally signed by a reluctant President in 1840 and became the law of the land.

It was estimated by contemporary observers that 95 percent of the tribe opposed the treaty; when an emigrating party was sent out in 1845, fewer than 250 elected to go, and most of the survivors of this little band returned to New York a few years later. The Society of Friends mobilized support for the Senecas; prominent attorneys, including Lewis Henry Morgan of Rochester, lobbied for them; lawsuits were filed against the Ogden Land Company. In 1842, a compromise was reached by which the company returned two of the reserves (Cattaraugus and Allegany) while retaining title to Buffalo Creek and Tonawanda. The Buffalo Creek Senecas moved to other reserves, but the Senecas of Tonawanda would not budge. In 1857, a small part of Tonawanda was bought back by the Senecas, along with the Tuscarora reservation. And decades later, the government paid the Senecas nearly $2 million for the million acres assigned to them in Kansas that it had opened to settlers without the consent of the tribe.

But even though the debacle at Buffalo Creek was partially reversed and the Senecas were allowed to remain on ancestral lands, the shock of the near-disaster produced a virtual revolution in Seneca society. The weakness of the traditional system of hereditary chiefs had become apparent, and in 1848 part of the tribe—the Allegany and Cattaraugus reservations—took advantage of a law passed by the New York State legislature that permitted tribal government by popularly elected chiefs. Calling themselves the "Seneca Nation," these two reserves combined to elect a joint chiefs' council and adopt a republican constitution. The population at Tonawanda—none of whose chiefs had signed the fraudulent treaty, although their names had been added to it without their knowledge—decided, however, to remain with the old way of selecting chiefs to represent the various matrilineal clans. And at the same time, the tribe generally experienced a revulsion against Christianity and Christians (of whom the Reverend John Schermerhorn was a very conspicuous example). As the Senecas' sympathetic resident missionary, Asher Wright, put it, "a dark cloud" overshadowed the influences of Christianity and blocked the work of saving souls:

> The pagan portion of the two Reservations availed themselves of the opportunity of union to build up and strengthen their cause against Christianity. Dances were multiplied, old ceremonies revived, and great effort was put forth to add interest and eclat to all their proceedings.

Nevertheless, Wright worked with others to reverse the Treaty of Buffalo Creek.

At Tonawanda, where the most traditional faction resided, a vigorous effort was made to revive both the old-time political structure and the old-time religion. The ancient League of the Iroquois, or Six Nations Confederacy, had fallen apart after the Revolution, when the Mohawks, Oneidas, and Cayugas went off to live in Canada, most of them on the Grand River in Ontario, leaving the Senecas and Onondagas behind in New York. And the Christians—at least at Cattaraugus and Allegany—had been attracting Indians to their services and even making converts. In 1845, a call went out to all the Iroquois reservations, in both New York and Ontario, to send delegates to a Six Nations meeting at Tonawanda, for the purpose of regenerating the confederacy and institutionalizing the "pagan" religion of Handsome Lake. Lewis Henry Morgan, who would publish his famous ethnography of the Iroquois in 1851, was given accounts of these Six Nations meetings by an educated young Seneca from Tonawanda, Ely S. Parker. Although the drive to reestablish the confederacy as a political force was not successful, the religious part of this post–Buffalo Creek cultural renaissance at Tonawanda was very successful indeed.

At the Six Nations meetings in 1845, a grandnephew of Handsome Lake, Jimmy Johnson, preached to the assembly his version of the old prophet's code (as he had been doing locally since the 1820s). Afterward, his version became the standard by which other preachers' renderings were judged. Although the grand gathering of delegates from many reservations was not continued, thereafter, in the fall, in a biennial circuit, Tonawanda-approved preachers traveled to each reservation where there were followers of the "Old Way of Handsome Lake," reciting the code in a four-day ceremony denominated the "Six Nations meeting" in recognition of the origin of the practice. Even today, traditionalists congregate in the longhouses to perform the annual calendar of ceremonies and to listen to the preachers recite the Code of Handsome Lake.

After the debacle of removal, with its bloodshed and suffering, the people who had spoken against the policy were joined by many more, who saw in it and its subsequent implementation by the Bureau of Indian Affairs a deadly combination of greed and self-righteousness.

The imputation of guilt may, however, stimulate precisely the reverse reaction: to blame the victim. This mechanism of defense may have been in part responsible for the popularity, in the 1840s and '50s, of "scientific" theories that declared not merely the inequality of races but their separate creation as distinct species. This polygenist view, advanced by the Philadelphia physician and phrenologist Samuel G. Morton and archaeologist and ethnologist Ephraim G. Squier and their numerous followers, explicitly rationalized not only Negro slavery but also Indian removal (and inevitable extinction). God, argued Morton, had given the white race "a decided and unquestioned superiority over all the nations of the earth." And in 1842 Morton wrote, apropos the removal of the racially inferior Native Americans:

Was it not for this same mental superiority, these happy climes which we now inhabit would yet be possessed by the wild and untutored Indian, and that soil which now rejoices the hearts of millions of freemen, would be yet overrun by lawless tribes of contending barbarians.

Morton's work was based on an examination of hundreds of Native American skulls, which he found to possess a smaller cranial capacity on average than those of whites, although far more than the skulls of adult blacks. The black cranium, asserted one of Morton's disciples, the eminent Harvard naturalist Louis Agassiz, housed a brain no larger than "the imperfect brain of a 7 month's infant in the womb of the white." Views such as these were widespread among believers in phrenology, like John S. Phillips of Rockdale, Pennsylvania, a close friend of Morton's, who no doubt debated them with his pious neighbors, Clementina Smith and Sophie DuPont, who maintained a warm interest in the welfare, both spiritual and material, of Indians, who were objects of their evangelical concern.

Although the credibility of the polygenist view among naturalists and physical anthropologists waned as creationism was replaced by evolutionism in scientific thought, the hunter thesis remained to influence the development of the disciplines of history and ethnology. Lewis Cass, who as we have seen was a principal articulator of the view that the Eastern Indians were hunters at heart, never wrote his grand treatise on the Native Americans. But his notes and essays and personal communications were to influence nineteenth-century scholars. Cass supplied Francis Parkman with notes and information that were used in the preparation of *The History of the Conspiracy of Pontiac* and others of his notable works on the colonial wars. Parkman's negative view of the Indian drew from other sources, too, including his friendship with Ephraim Squier (which led Parkman to foresee the future extinction of the Indians as a result of biological inferiority) and from his interpretation of his personal experiences with Indians in New England and the West.

Another result of the removal controversy was to somewhat warp the infant science of ethnology. Lewis Henry Morgan, whom we have already met as a defender of Iroquois land rights and as the author of what has been called the first modern ethnography, is generally conceded to be the father of American anthropology. But between Cass and Morgan stands Henry R. Schoolcraft, whom we have also met before as agent to the Chippewa in northern Michigan and as commissioner to arrange with them a major removal treaty in 1836. Cass was Schoolcraft's employer, mentor, and traveling companion; Schoolcraft became Cass's literary alter ego, carrying forward his mentor's plan for studies of the Indian languages, customs, and traditions. Schoolcraft believed implicitly in Cass's concept of the hunter state and in the psychological lag that prevented Indian men (Schoolcraft married a well-educated Indian woman) from embracing Western civilization.

In 1845, Schoolcraft was invited to address the third annual meeting of Morgan's club of amateur ethnologists in Rochester. There he delivered a eulogistic talk on the Iroquois and their confederacy, anticipating in some ways the future work of Morgan in his emphasis on the importance of matrilineal kinship in the Iroquois social organization, and on the political wisdom displayed in the principle of tribal confederacy. But he still considered the Iroquois to be exemplars of the hunter state. Two years later, Schoolcraft published his *Notes on the Iroquois*, based in part on his visit to the reservations in New York, and here—as we noted earlier—he recognized that two-thirds of the men were farmers and only a third remained as "half-hunters."

Morgan, of course, knew Schoolcraft personally, and at least knew of Cass by reputation; in December 1845, not long after Schoolcraft's visit, he invited Cass to become a member of the Rochester club of Iroquoianists. And his *League of the Ho-de-no-sau-nee or Iroquois* presented Iroquois men in a somber Cassian light, at least insofar as their present condition and prospects for improvement were conceived.

The passion of the red man for the hunter life has proved to be a principle too deeply inwrought, to be controlled by efforts of legislation. His government, if one was sought to be established, must have conformed to this irresistible tendency of his mind, this inborn sentiment; otherwise it would have been disregarded. The effect of this powerful principle has been to enchain the tribes of North America to their primitive state.

But Morgan differed sharply from Cass and Schoolcraft in regard to the desirability of a segregationist removal policy, which he considered to be not only immoral but also ineffective in ameliorating the Indians' condition. In the concluding chapter of the Iroquois book, reflecting on "The Future Destiny of the Indian," he deplored the fact that "during the last sixty years . . . the whole territory east of the Mississippi, with inconsiderable exceptions, has been swept from the Indian." And he criticized the recent removal treaties with the Seminoles, the Cherokees, and the Iroquois as examples of "sharp-sighted diplomacy, or ungenerous coercion, and of grievous injustice." Morgan, unlike Cass, felt that education in the arts and crafts of civilization, and freedom from bureaucratic supervision, could save the Indians from otherwise inevitable extinction.

Morgan also differed from Cass in regard to the importance of female agriculture in the aboriginal economy of the Eastern Indians. Their subsistence "rested chiefly upon the industry, and therefore upon the natural kindness of the Indian woman; who, by the cultivation of the maize, and their other plants, and the gathering of the wild fruits, provided the principal part of their subsistence . . ." And later, in *Ancient Society* (first published in 1877), Morgan placed the Eastern tribes in the "Lower Stage of Barbarism," defining them as "partially Village Indians' (i.e., near the status of the Pueblos), markedly above the hunter state of savagism.

Cass, Schoolcraft, and Morgan, whatever their differences, set an intellectual agenda that American anthropology, centered in the Smithsonian Institution's Bureau of American Ethnology, followed well into the twentieth century. The notion of progressive stages of cultural evolution, and concern with the conditions and difficulties of advancement from one stage to another (from the hunter state to civilization, in the case of the Indians) occupied a number of the BAE researchers. One of the agency's main tasks was to prepare a detailed history of the land cessions by which the natives conveyed their land to the United States government. In 1899, the definitive work on this subject was published, Josiah Royce's *Indian Land Cessions in the United States*, containing maps and an abstract of every land-cession treaty to date. The introduction was written by another BAE researcher, Cyrus Thomas. Thomas quoted with approval from an 1823 decision of the U.S. Supreme Court concerning the nature of "Indian title":

> discovery [by Europeans] gave an exclusive right to extinguish the Indian title of occupancy, either by purchase or by conquest . . . We will not enter into the controversy, whether agriculturists, merchants, and manufacturers, have a right on abstract principle, to expel hunters from the territory they possess, or to contract their limits . . . The tribes of Indians inhabiting this country were fierce savages, whose occupation was war, and whose subsistence was drawn chiefly from the forest.

And in the *Handbook of American Indians North of Mexico*, in her articles on "Governmental Policy" and "Reservations," Alice Fletcher, the distinguished BAE ethnologist and sometime agent of the Bureau of Indian Affairs, was still in 1905 able to write that the policy of requiring land cessions and confining the Indians to reservations "was a most important step in the process of leading the natives to abandon the hunter stage and to depend for their subsistence on agriculture and home industries." Quotations of this sort could be multiplied endlessly.

The preoccupation of anthropologists with classifying native peoples according to a scheme of stages of progress toward civilization faded in the early years of the twentieth century. Led by Franz Boas and the Columbia school of anthropology, the new focus of research was the reconstruction of the authentic, aboriginal culture, and the tracing of the unique history of each tribal group. But one may suspect that the theory of the hunter state, and the stereotype of the Indians as "wandering barbarians" at heart, still survives in law, in litigation, and in the unwritten traditions of state and federal bureaucracies.

But perhaps the most enduring relic of the removal policy has been the Bureau of Indian Affairs. It will be recalled that in 1830 Jackson had fired Thomas McKenney, the Superintendent of the Bureau of Indian Affairs. His office had been chiefly concerned with administering the old Trade and Intercourse Acts, which more or less regulated commerce with the Indians and disbursed the Education Fund. In 1834, a bill, drawn up with the advice of Lewis Cass and William Clark, was passed by Congress and signed by Jackson, creating a new and expanded Bureau of Indian Affairs, still within the War Department. In 1849, as the Bureau of Indian Affairs, it was transferred from the War Department to the Department of Interior, where it has remained to this day.

The responsibilities, and the size and complexity, of the Bureau of Indian Affairs expanded enormously over the years as it took over the management and support of more and more aspects of Native American life. By 1907, when the Indian territory ceased to exist and the state of Oklahoma was created in its stead, the bureau was spending $10 million annually for various activities on the reservations, including public schools for native children, and employed about five thousand people. Agents were political appointees selected for party loyalty rather than expertise in Native American affairs. The agents were virtual dictators on their reservations, literally exercising the powers of life and death. Their duties included the disbursement of annuities, distribution of rations, superintendency of the schools, removal of intruders, the "preservation of order" (directing the reservation police), and supervision of the bureau's employees. A partial list of employee categories gives an idea of the extent to which the bureau penetrated the life of the reservation: schoolteachers, clerks, police, farmers, carpenters, blacksmiths, millers, butchers, teamsters, herders, watchmen, interpreters, engineers, physicians . . .

Obviously the Bureau of Indian Affairs, vast, sprawling, a model of bureaucracy run amuck, offered opportunities for all sorts of mismanagement and corruption, and numerous complaints were made. President Grant, and others, tried to reform agency rule by appointing former military officers, or even officers currently in service; he even made General Ely S. Parker (the Seneca Indian who had helped Lewis Henry Morgan begin his study of the Iroquois) the head of the bureau. Parker, who was a civil engineer by profession, had served on the staff of General Grant during the Civil War and had been present at Lee's surrender at Appomatox. But Congress passed a law prohibiting the practice of appointing military officers to administrative positions in civilian agencies. The abuses of the reservation system gave new life to the old idea of "incorporation," the policy of making the Indians full citizens of the states and the nation, owning land in fee simple as individuals, like other Americans, instead of confining them to reservations under the control of a corrupt bureaucracy that claimed to be "civilizing" the Indians when, in fact, they were merely exploiting them. The incorporation idea had been loudly voiced by one of Andrew Jackson's chief political rivals, William Crawford of Georgia, who served as Secretary of War during Madison's administration, and who questioned Jackson's aggressive pursuit of a removal policy in the years after the War of 1812.

Now the incorporation idea was linked to the notion of distributing reservation land to individuals and in effect abolishing both the reservations and the Bureau of Indian Affairs, "mainstreaming" (to use a later bit of jargon) the Native Americans. The Board of Indian Commissioners, established by President Grant in 1869, began a series of investigations of conditions on the reservations, and private organizations of prominent persons concerned for Indian welfare joined forces in pressing for a more enlightened system. In 1887, Congress passed the Dawes Act, named for Senator Henry Dawes, chairman of the Senate's Committee on Indian Affairs. This "severalty act" provided for the allotment of tribal lands to Indians who wished to hold their property in fee simple and were prepared to accept the rights and duties of citizenship. Although some tribal lands were in principle permitted to remain in the joint ownership of those who did not wish to give up their tribal identification, the act looked toward the ending of the reservation system. This aim was further pursued in the so-called Curtis Act of 1898, named for Congressman Charles Curtis, a Native American who later became Vice President under Herbert Hoover, that extinguished tribal governments—which tended to oppose allotments—and made all Indians citizens of their respective states and of the United States. The Severalty Act of 1887 temporarily exempted the Five Civilized Tribes, but in 1893 Dawes became the chairman of a commission to reorganize the Indian territory and secure the agreement of the chiefs to allotment and to the extinguishment of tribal title. The work of enrolling the members of the Five Tribes began in 1906, and the next year Oklahoma became a state.

The allotment system, however well intended, did not serve the Native Americans of Oklahoma well. Although each man, woman, and child was entitled to a portion of the tribal land, supposedly sufficient for each individual or family to support themselves by farming, and although these allotments were to be held in trust for twenty-five years, in order to prevent hasty sale of properties, and only then were to be converted into fee-simple titles, relatively few Indian families had the capital or the experience to operate a family farm successfully. Poverty, ill health, little or no formal education, low morale were the fate of many, and the allotment system itself eventually came under attack by friends of the Indians. It simply resulted in the progressive destruction of tribal solidarity and identity, and the loss of their land. Eventually the government's policy was again reversed, under the aegis of the New Deal, by the Indian Reorganization Act of 1934, which provided for the renewed recognition of the tribes as viable political and economic entities and facilitated the reacquisition by the tribes of land alienated under allotment.

But the pendulum of an ambivalent Indian policy keeps swinging. In the 1950s, a Termination Act brought forth again the goal of incorporation as the national intent. Opposed by the very tribal populations it was intended to free from the shackles of reservation life, it in turn was rescinded. Two hundred years of national indecision about how the United States should deal with its Native Americans have not come to an end.

APPENDIX A
EXCERPT FROM JACKSON'S MESSAGE
TO CONGRESS
DECEMBER 8, 1829

The condition and ulterior destiny of the Indian Tribes within the limits of some of our States, have become objects of much interest and importance. It has long been the policy of Government to introduce among them the arts of civilization, in the hope of gradually reclaiming them from a wandering life. This policy has, however, been coupled with another, wholly incompatible with its success. Professing a desire to civilize and settle them, we have, at the same time, lost no opportunity to purchase their lands, and thrust them further into the wilderness. By this means they have not only been kept in a wandering state, but been led to look upon us as unjust and indifferent to their fate. Thus, though lavish in its expenditures upon the subject, Government has constantly defeated its own policy; and the Indians, in general, receding further and further to the West, have retained their savage habits. A portion, however, of the Southern tribes, having mingled much with the whites, and made some progress in the arts of civilized life, have lately attempted to erect an independent government, within the limits of Georgia and Alabama. These States, claiming to be the only Sovereigns within their territories, extended their laws over the Indians; which induced the latter to call upon the United States for protection.

Under these circumstances, the question presented was, whether the General Government had a right to sustain those people in their pretensions? The Constitution declares, that "no new State shall be formed or erected within the jurisdiction of any other State," without the consent of its legislature. If the General Government is not permitted to tolerate the erection of a confederate State within the territory of one of the members of this Union, against her consent; much less could it allow a foreign and independent government to establish itself there. Georgia became a member of the Confederacy which eventuated in our Federal Union, as a sovereign State, always asserting her claim to certain limits; which having been originally defined in her colonial charter, and subsequently recognised in the treaty of peace, she has ever since continued to enjoy, except as they have been circumscribed by her own voluntary transfer of a portion of her territory to the United States, in the articles of cession of 1802. Alabama was admitted into the Union on the same footing with the original States, with boundaries which were prescribed by Congress. There is no constitutional, conventional, or legal provision, which allows them less power over the Indians within their borders, than is possessed by Maine or New York. Would the People of Maine permit the Penobscot tribe to erect an Independent Government within their State? and unless they did, would it not be the duty of the General Government to support them in resisting such a measure? Would the People of New York permit each remnant of the Six Nations within her borders, to declare itself an independent people under the protection of the United States? Could the Indians establish a separate republic on each of their reservations in Ohio? and if they were so disposed, would it be the duty of this Government to protect them in the attempt? If the principle involved in the obvious answer to these questions be abandoned, it will follow that the objects of this Government are reversed; and that it has become a part of its duty to aid in destroying the States which it was established to protect.

Actuated by this view of the subject, I informed the Indians inhabiting parts of Georgia and Alabama, that their attempt to establish an independent government would not be countenanced by the Executive of the United States; and advised them to emigrate beyond the Mississippi, or submit to the laws of those States.

Our conduct towards these people is deeply interesting to our national character. Their present condition, contrasted with what they once were, makes a most powerful appeal to our sympathies. Our ancestors found them the uncontrolled possessors of these vast regions. By persuasion and force, they have been made to retire from river to river, and from mountain to mountain; until some of the tribes have become extinct, and others have left but remnants, to preserve, for a while, their once terrible names. Surrounded by the whites, with their arts of civilization, which, by destroying the resources of the savage, doom him to weakness and decay; the fate of the Mohegan, the Narragansett, and the Delaware, is fast overtaking the Choctaw, the Cherokee, and the Creek. That this fate surely awaits them, if they remain within the limits of the States, does not admit of a doubt. Humanity and national honor demand that every effort should be made to avert so great a calamity. It is too late to inquire whether it was just in the United States to include them and their territory within the bounds of new States whose limits they could control. That step cannot be retraced. A State cannot be dismembered by Congress, or restricted in the exercise of her constitutional power. But the people of those States, and of every State, actuated by feelings of justice and a regard for our national honor, submit to you the interesting question, whether something cannot be done, consistently with the rights of the States, to preserve this much injured race?

As a means of effecting this end, I suggest, for your consideration, the propriety of setting apart an ample district West of the Mississippi, and without the limits of any State or Territory, now formed, to be guarantied to the Indian tribes, as long as they shall occupy it: each tribe having a distinct control over the portion designated for its use. There they may be secured in the enjoyment of governments of their own choice, subject to no other control from the United States than such as may be necessary to preserve peace on the frontier, and between the several tribes. There the benevolent may endeavor to teach them the arts of civilization; and, by promoting union and harmony among them, to raise up an interesting commonwealth, destined to perpetuate the race, and to attest the humanity and justice of this Government.

This emigration should be voluntary: for it would be as cruel as unjust to compel the aborigines to abandon the graves of their fathers, and seek a home in a distant land. But they should be distinctly informed that, if they remain within the limits of the States, they must be subject to their laws. In return for their obedience, as individuals, they will, without doubt, be protected in the enjoyment of those possessions which they have improved by their industry. But it seems to me visionary to suppose, that, in this state of things, claims can be allowed on tracts of country on which they have neither dwelt nor made improvements, merely because they have seen them from the mountain, or passed them in the chace. Submitting to the laws of the States, and receiving, like other citizens, protection in their persons and property, they will, ere long, become merged in the mass of our population.

The Text of the Removal Act

An Act to Provide for an Exchange of Lands with the Indians Residing in any of the States or Territories, and for their Removal West of the River Mississippi.

Be it enacted by the Senate and House of Representatives of the United States of America, in Congress assembled, That it shall and may be lawful for the President of the United States to cause so much of any territory belonging to the United States, west of the river Mississippi, not included in any state or organized territory, and to which the Indian title has been extinguished, as he may judge necessary, to be divided into a suitable number of districts, for the reception of such tribes or nations of Indians as may choose to exchange the lands where they now reside, and remove there; and to cause each of said districts to be so described by natural or artificial marks, as to be easily distinguished from every other.

SECTION II

And be it further enacted, That it shall and may be lawful for the President to exchange any or all of such districts, so to be laid off and described, with any tribe or nation of Indians now residing within the limits of any of the states or territories, and with which the United States have existing treaties, for the whole or any part or portion of the territory claimed and occupied by such tribe or nation, within the bounds of any one or more of the states or territories, where the land claimed and occupied by the Indians, is owned by the United States, or the United States are bound to the state within which it lies to extinguish the Indian claim thereto.

SECTION III

And be it further enacted, That in the making of any such exchange or exchanges, it shall and may be lawful for the President solemnly to assure the tribe or nation with which the exchange is made, that the United States will forever secure and guaranty to them, and their heirs or successors, the country so exchanged with them; and if they prefer it, that the United States will cause a patent or grant to be made and executed to them for the same: Provided always, That such lands shall revert to the United States, if the Indians become extinct, or abandon the same.

SECTION IV

And be it further enacted, That if, upon any of the lands now occupied by the Indians, and to be exchanged for, there should be such improvements as add value to the land claimed by any individual or individuals of such tribes or nations, it shall and may be lawful for the President to cause such value to be ascertained by appraisement or otherwise, and to cause such ascertained value to be paid to the person or persons rightfully claiming such improvements. And upon the payment of such valuation, the improvements so valued and paid for, shall pass to the United States, and possession shall not afterwards be permitted to any of the same tribe.

SECTION V

And be it further enacted, That upon the making of any such exchange as is contemplated by this act, it shall and may be lawful for the President to cause such aid and assistance to be furnished to the emigrants as may be necessary and proper to enable them to remove to, and settle in, the country for which they may have exchanged; and also, to give them such aid and assistance as may be necessary for their support and subsistence for the first year after their removal.

SECTION VI

And be it further enacted, That it shall and may be lawful for the President to cause such tribe or nation to be protected, at their new residence, against all interruption or disturbance from any other tribe or nation of Indians, or from any other person or persons whatever.

SECTION VII

And be it further enacted, That it shall and may be lawful for the President to have the same superintendence and care over any tribe or nation in the country to which they may remove, as contemplated by this act, that he is now authorized to have over them at their present places of residence: Provided, That nothing in this act contained shall be construed as authorizing or directing the violation of any existing treaty between the United States and any of the Indian tribes.

SECTION VIII

And be it further enacted, That for the purpose of giving effect to the provisions of this act, the sum of five hundred thousand dollars is hereby appropriated, to be paid out of any money in the treasury, not otherwise appropriated.

Approved, May 28, 1830.

A Note on Sources

There exists a vast literature on Native Americans and their relation to the European colonies and later the United States. This bibliographic note aims only to draw the reader's attention to a few of the major reference works, published compilations of primary documents, and useful secondary studies by reliable historians and anthropologists.

The two standard encyclopedias of Native American cultures and history are: F. W. Hodge, ed., *Handbook of American Indians North of Mexico*, 2 vols. (Washington: Bulletin 30, Bureau of American Ethnology, 1907–10), still useful as an alphabetically organized compendium of tribal sketches, biographies, and brief essays on various subjects; and William C. Sturtevant, ed., *Handbook of North American Indians*, 20 vols. (Washington: Smithsonian Institution). Some of the volumes of the new *Handbook* are still in press, including the one on the Indians of the Southeast, but two have been useful in the preparation of this book: Bruce C. Trigger, ed., *Northeast* (Vol. 15, 1978), and Wilcomb E. Washburn, ed., *History of Indian–White Relations* (Vol. 4, 1988). Indispensable in any study of land transfers is Charles C. Royce, *Indian Land Cessions in the United States*, Part 2 of the 18th Annual Report of the Bureau of American Ethnology for the Years 1896–1897 (Washington: Government Printing Office, 1899). Royce provides abstracts of the land cession treaties in chronological order and maps, state by state, showing the boundaries of each cession.

No comprehensive one-volume survey of the Indians of the Northeast is available, apart from the *Handbook*, but for the Southeast there is Charles Hudson, *The Southeastern Indians* (Knoxville: University of Tennessee Press, 1976), an anthropological summary, and R. S. Cotterill, *The Southern Indians: The Story of the Civilized Tribes Before Removal* (Norman: University of Oklahoma Press, 1954), a historian's detailed account of events leading up to 1830. An important compilation is Charles J. Kappler, ed., *Indian Affairs: Laws and Treaties*, 5 vols. (Washington: Government Printing Office, 1904–41; reprinted, AMS Press, 1971), but the most usable compendium is Wilcomb E. Washburn, ed., *The American Indian and the United States: A Documentary History*, 4 vols. (New York: Random House, 1973), containing reprints of treaties, congressional debates, laws, reports of the Indian commissioners, legal decisions, and much else. For one contemporary survey of the Native Americans of the East in the years before removal, see Jedidiah Morse, *A Report to the Secretary of War of the United States, on Indian Affairs* . . . (New Haven: S. Converse, 1822).

Several historians have dealt with the course of federal Indian policy toward the Eastern Indians, beginning with Annie H. Abel, *The History of Events Resulting in Indian Consolidation West of the Mississippi*, Annual Report of the American Historical Association for the Year 1906 (Washington, 1908). Recent studies of related policy issues are two books by Francis Paul Prucha, *American Indian Policy in the Formative Years: The Indian Trade and Intercourse Acts, 1790–1834* (Cambridge: Harvard University Press, 1962), and *The Great Father* (Lincoln: University of Nebraska Press, 1984). See also Ronald M. Satz, *American Indian Policy in the Jacksonian Era* (Lincoln: University of Nebraska Press, 1975). An important compilation of legal material is Felix Cohen, *Handbook of Federal Indian Law* (Albuquerque: University of New Mexico Press, 1971). This edition reprints Cohen's original 1942 publication, not the mutilated revision that appeared in 1958, when "termination" was in vogue in Washington.

The classic studies of Indian removal and its aftermath are, of course, Grant Foreman's two books, *Indian Removal: The Emigration of the Five Civilized Tribes of Indians* (Norman: University of Oklahoma Press, 1932) and *The Five Civilized Tribes* (Norman: University of Oklahoma Press, 1934), and Angie Debo's *And Still the Waters Run: The Betrayal of the Five Civilized Tribes* (Princeton: Princeton University Press, 1940). There are also more specialized studies of the removal of individual tribes: for the Cherokees, John Ehle, *Trail of Tears: The Rise and Fall of the Cherokee Nation* (New York: Doubleday/Anchor Books, 1988); for the Creeks, Mary E. Young, *Redskins, Ruffleshirts, and Rednecks: Indian Allotments in Alabama and Mississippi, 1830–1860* (Norman: University of Oklahoma Press, 1961); for the Choctaws, Arthur H. DeRosier, Jr., *The Removal of the Choctaw Indians* (Knoxville: University of Tennessee Press, 1970); for the Chickasaws, Arrell N. Gibson, *The Chickasaws* (Norman: University of Oklahoma Press, 1971); and for the Seminoles, John K. Mahon, *History of the Second Seminole War, 1835–1842* (Gainesville: University of Florida Press, 1967), and William C. Sturtevant, "Creek into Seminole," in Eleanor Leacock and Nancy Lurie, eds., *North American Indians in Historical Perspective* (Prospect Heights: Waveland Press, 1978).

What might be called the intellectual history of Indian–white relations has received a good deal of attention from historians. Of particular use in this study was Robert E. Bieder, *Science Encounters the Indian, 1820–1880* (Norman: University of Oklahoma Press, 1986), which draws attention to the role of Lewis Cass and his influence on early anthropology. Still valuable is Roy Harvey Pearce's well-known work, *The Savages of America: A Study of the Indian and the Idea of Civilization* (Baltimore: Johns Hopkins University Press, 1953). More recent surveys and compilations include Robert F. Berkhofer, Jr., *The White Man's Indian: Images of the American Indian from Columbus to the Present* (New York: Alfred A. Knopf, 1978), and Wilcomb E. Washburn, ed., *The Indian and the White Man* (Garden City: Anchor Books, 1964).

And finally, there are biographical studies of several of the principal figures in the removal process. Many of the important Native Americans involved, and of course the whites, are the subject of brief sketches in the *Dictionary of American Biography*. Information about the life of John Ross may be found in Gary E. Moulton, *John Ross, Cherokee Chief* (Athens: University of Georgia Press, 1978). Lewis Cass's career is described in Frank B. Woodford, *Lewis Cass: The Last Jeffersonian* (New Brunswick: Rutgers University Press, 1950). The long-suffering Indian superintendent is the subject of Herman J. Viola's *Thomas L. McKenney: Architect of America's Early Indian Policy 1816–1830* (Chicago: Swallow Press, 1974). And, of course, Andrew Jackson has had a number of biographers. Of most value in the preparation of this book have been Paul Rogin, *Fathers and Children: Andrew Jackson and the Subjugation of the American Indian* (New York: Alfred A. Knopf, 1975), and Robert V. Remini, *Andrew Jackson and the Course of American Freedom, 1822–1832* (New York: Harper & Row, 1981); see also the condensation of Remini's three-volume biography, *The Life of Andrew Jackson* (New York: Harper & Row, 1988).

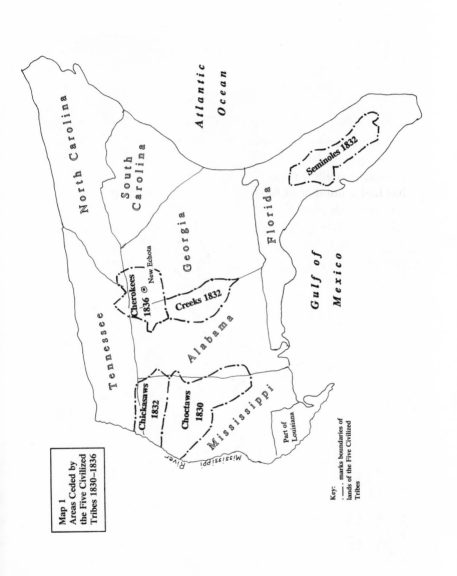

Map 1
Areas Ceded by
the Five Civilized
Tribes 1830–1836

North Carolina

South Carolina

Atlantic Ocean

Georgia

Tennessee

Florida

Seminoles 1832

Gulf of Mexico

Cherokees 1836 ⊙ New Echota

Creeks 1832

Alabama

Chickasaws 1832

Choctaws 1830

Mississippi

Mississippi River

Part of Louisiana

Key:
─ ∙ ─ marks boundaries of
lands of the Five Civilized
Tribes

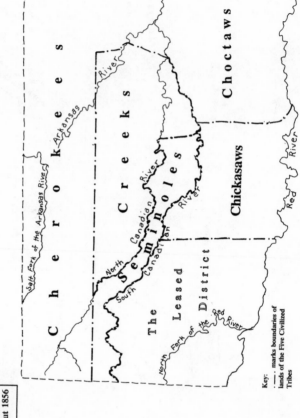

Map 2
Lands Occupied by the
Five Civilized Tribes in
Indian Territory (later
Oklahoma)—about 1856

Cherokees

Creeks

Seminoles

Choctaws

Chickasaws

The Leased District

Arkansas River

Salt Fork of the Arkansas River

Canadian River

North Canadian River

South Canadian River

North Fork of the Red River

Red River

Key:
─ ∙ ─ ∙ ─ marks boundaries of
lands of the Five Civilized
Tribes

INDEX

Brainerd, David, 35, 59, 60
Brant, Joseph, 27, 35
Brown, David, 59
buffalo, 17
Buffalo Creek reservation, 109–11
Bureau of Indian Affairs, 11, 59, 112, 116, 117–20
Butler, Elizur, 75–76, 103

Calhoun, John C., 39, 64, 69, 76
California, 105
Cameron, Simon, 107
Canada, 24, 25, 35, 37, 44–45, 78, 111
Cass, Lewis, 40, 41–48, 61, 67, 73–74, 81, 84, 86, 87, 89, 91, 108, 113–15, 117
Catawba Indians, 105
Catlin, George, 100
Cattaraugus reservation, 110, 111
Cayuga Indians, 21, 111
Central America, 15, 19
ceremonies, Indian, 15–21, 111–12
Cherokee Advocate, The (newspaper), 103
Cherokee Indians, 3, 4, 9–10, 16, 22, 25–27, 29, 50–54, 58–61, 67, 74, 77; in aftermath of removal policy, 102–5; constitution of, 10, 62, 64; Eastern, 90–94; land cessions of 1763–89, 26–27; land cessions of 1814–30, 50–56, 63–64; trans-Mississippi removal of, 73–74, 88–94; Western, 88, 90; white customs adopted by, 58–62
Cherokee Phoenix, The (newspaper), 60, 75, 89, 91

Cheyenne Indians, 105
Chickasaw Indians, 16, 20, 25, 29, 39, 51, 52, 53, 58–61, 74, 77, 94, 103–4, 105; in aftermath of removal policy, 102–5; trans-Mississippi removal of, 81–83
Chippewa Indians, 106, 108, 114
Choctaw Indians, 16, 22, 25, 29, 52, 53, 58, 59–61, 74, 94, 103–4; 105; in aftermath of removal policy, 102–5; trans-Mississippi removal of, 74, 77–83
Christianity, 34–36, 57, 61, 67–68, 70, 110–11
Civil War, 101, 104, 105, 118
Clark, William, 40, 117
Clay, Henry, 47, 68
coal, 7
Coffee, John, 5, 9, 51–52, 54, 73, 76–78, 82, 95
Columbus, Christopher, 16
Comanche Indians, 102, 105
Congress, U.S., 3, 32, 36, 38, 39–41, 55, 76, 104, 117, 118–19; debate over Removal Act, 64–70; *see also* House of Representatives, U.S.; Senate, U.S.
"Conspiracy of Pontiac," 25–26
Constitution, U.S., 62, 63, 68, 89
Cooper, James Fenimore, 36, 46; *The Last of the Mohicans*, 36; *The Pioneers*, 36
cotton, 4, 6–11, 59–62, 64; British, 7; Southern, 6–11, 57, 59–62
Crawford, William, 51–52, 64, 118
Creek Indians, 4, 5, 9, 16, 25, 27, 28–29, 50–54, 58–61, 74, 77, 90, 94, 95, 98, 104; in